DECADE OF CHANGE

MANAGING IN TIMES OF UNCERTAINTY

Edited by

GEOFFREY BREWER | BARB SANFORD

GALLUP PRESS
1251 Avenue of the Americas
23rd Floor
New York, NY 10020

Library of Congress Control Number: 2011921787
ISBN: 978-1-59562-053-8

First Printing: 2011
10 9 8 7 6 5 4 3 2 1

BESTSELLERS FROM GALLUP PRESS

TABLE OF CONTENTS

INTRODUCTION

You no doubt remember the much-anticipated, much-dreaded Y2K "crisis." The world's computers were going to freeze at the stroke of midnight, January 1, 2000. Stored information would be wiped out around the globe. Power grids would go dark, markets would tumble, chaos would ensue. Planes might even fall from the sky.

How quaint that non-crisis seems now. New Year's Day 2000 turned out to be a tranquil affair just about everywhere. If anything, relative peace, calm, and goodwill prevailed.

But maybe we were onto something. Maybe we just *sensed*, in some nameless, inchoate way, that vast, threatening, even frightening changes loomed. Perhaps our fretting was justified, if simply misplaced. It sure seems that way now.

To say that the new millennium brought with it staggering changes, even if not right at the moment we anticipated, is to understate. Planes did crash into buildings and, indeed, fall from the sky. Markets tumbled . . . and tumbled and tumbled. Chaos, in many parts of the world, has ensued.

In many ways, the world got its Y2K crisis. But it was spread out over a decade, and we live with the implications today.

But while 9/11, the wars in Iraq and Afghanistan, turmoil in the Middle East and Asia, the warmest decade on record, and the collapse of global financial markets tend to be discussed as political and economic issues, they're also management and leadership issues. For as any forward-thinking senior executive and organizational leader knows, the world's problems very quickly become business problems.

Employees and customers fear terrorism and instability, and they act accordingly, perhaps irrationally. Some valued employees, such as those in the military reserves or the National Guard, get sent off to war. And a financial collapse, such as the one we endured in the fall of 2008, devastates people and profits; dramatically shrinks or wipes out markets;

and leaves in its wake layoffs, downsizing, uncertainty, and dramatically altered expectations.

Change is often an abstract concept, discussed in business conferences and academic seminars. But it's been all too real this past decade.

The momentousness of change during the past 10 years has inspired us, editors at the *Gallup Management Journal*, to review how we covered and evaluated events during this period; how we tried to make sense of rapid change right as it was unfolding; and most importantly, how our most visionary people, as well as the great minds with whom Gallup regularly associates, helped organizational leaders navigate the most tumultuous years in recent memory.

In these pages, you'll find insights and wisdom into how to manage, and make the most of, change. Nobel Prize winner Daniel Kahneman probes the nature of decision making. Lieutenant General Russel Honoré of Hurricane Katrina fame offers leadership lessons he applied in the crucible of crisis. Vinton Cerf, one of the creators of the Internet, peers into the Web's future. Visionary executive Ray Anderson shows how to make green while going green. Gallup Chairman and CEO Jim Clifton reveals what everyone on the globe most wants. And a host of other executives and thinkers tackle everything from mitigating the fear of layoffs and promoting wellbeing in the workplace to building customer engagement amid the post-crash "new normal."

You'll hear from some of the best business and organizational minds, steering leaders through the various crises of the past decade and helping find a way forward to what we all hope will be a brighter and more prosperous future. *Decade of Change* is more than a look backward; it is a roadmap for what lies ahead.

Geoffrey Brewer

Barb Sanford

January 2011

GLOBAL CHANGES

WHAT WERE THEY THINKING?

An interview with Nobel Prize Winner Daniel Kahneman
by Jennifer Robison

January 13, 2005

Daniel Kahneman, Ph.D., has started a quiet little revolution — one that may wind up blasting a big hole in the foundation of economics. For centuries, economists have based most of their theories on the "rational-agent model," which assumes that people make reasonable decisions and do simple cost/benefit analyses on the things they buy. But they don't. Dr. Kahneman's research shows that, probably more often than not, individual decisions are based on perception, context, and faulty reasoning — all of which can be manipulated.

Interestingly, Dr. Kahneman is not an economist. He's a psychologist — Eugene Higgins Professor of Psychology at Princeton University; a professor of public affairs at the Woodrow Wilson School; and a Gallup senior scientist, one of a cadre of leading scientists who lend their expertise to Gallup research.

But Kahneman belongs to an even more rarefied group: In October 2002, The Royal Swedish Academy of Sciences awarded him the Nobel Prize in economics "for having integrated insights from psychological research into economic science, especially concerning human judgment and decision-making under uncertainty."

Kahneman's insights are as relevant to the global economic scale as they are to the average shampoo purchase. What we think we know about our own decisions is wrong, and what we thought we knew about economics may be just as wrong. And anyone who hopes to create revenue for an organization will do well to learn from what Kahneman has discovered.

In this interview, Dr. Kahneman discusses how businesspeople should make high-level decisions, when and how people fall prey to cognitive illusions, and why everything *always* depends on context.

Gallup Management Journal: A lot of your research has centered on the way people think, and you've identified two broad categories: intuition and reasoning. What's the difference?

Dr. Kahneman: Intuitive thoughts are those that come to you quickly and effortlessly, whereas reasoning is something that you've got to work at and is characteristically effortful and slower. Everyone does both — thinks intuitively and reasons. But usually we're guided by and operate at the intuitive level. We don't slow ourselves down to reason carefully most of the time.

GMJ: Is that true for every facet of life, from decisions about what we're going to have for supper to which car should we buy?

Dr. Kahneman: Well, that's tricky. We use intuitive thinking more often than we realize, but which car to buy is a much more complicated operation. In such a case, you have intuitive wishes, and you have an initial emotional response. Buying a car is never a purely intuitive, spontaneous, impulsive thing; you reason about the car. But the reasoning is superimposed on an emotional attitude.

GMJ: How often is that first system of thinking, intuitive thinking, wrong?

Dr. Kahneman: It's fine most of the time. You know, we're very highly skilled in what we do. Whenever you develop a skill, it becomes part of that intuitive system of thought. You drive your car intuitively — you don't think about every single operation as you do it — and we're awfully good at that. What is remarkable is that people don't check themselves. We give answers without thinking. And most of the time we're okay. But sometimes that habit of mind gets us into trouble.

GMJ: On the other hand, if you checked every decision you ever made . . .

Dr. Kahneman: . . . you couldn't possibly live. It would just slow you down too much. You know, we've got to act, and we are, in general, very skilled at what we do.

GMJ: One of the reasons that you were awarded the Nobel Prize is you showed that the rational-agent model of economics — that people buy things based on a careful, reasoned cost/benefit analysis, not intuition or emotion — isn't necessarily correct, right?

Dr. Kahneman: Sort of. The line of research that I've engaged in is called the study of bounded rationality. That is, people are reasonable, but their minds are limited. So it's not that people are necessarily driven by emotion — they're driven by mental computations that are incomplete or inaccurate, and they're susceptible to what we call cognitive illusions. And that's a different thing than being driven by emotions.

GMJ: What's a cognitive illusion?

Dr. Kahneman: It's an impression that you get at the intuitive, but not necessarily emotional, level that is wrong or misleading. Cognitive illusions are difficult to shake, and often we get them because these impressions come from accessibility. Accessibility refers to impressions based on the most accessible thought or explanation. For example, an easy question is one where the answer comes easily to mind — it's highly accessible. The answers to difficult questions are not so easily accessible.

GMJ: Are some thoughts more accessible than others?

Dr. Kahneman: Oh, yes. There are certain ideas that come to mind very easily for various reasons. If you're in a bad mood, then thoughts of bad events come easily to mind — the world will now seem like a more dangerous place, and you'll be more pessimistic about the future. Just being in a bad mood changes the accessibility of a whole lot of other thoughts. It's harder to imagine people laughing and smiling, and it's easier to imagine wakes and funerals.

GMJ: So if you can change someone's mood . . .

Dr. Kahneman: Oh, you can change many things about their beliefs about the world.

GMJ: How easy is it to do that?

Dr. Kahneman: Very easy. I'll give you an example from an experiment. A researcher had someone lurk around a phone booth, posing as a survey researcher. Half the time, he put a quarter in the phone booth. And so half the people who used the phone found a quarter, so they got the telephone call for free. Then, when they came out, the researcher asked them to answer a survey. Among other things, he asked them how happy they were with their lives in general. People who just found a quarter in the phone booth were much likelier to say that they were much happier with their life in general these days than the people who didn't find a quarter.

So even a small event that makes you feel lucky for just a few minutes will make thoughts of happiness much more accessible. If your first thought is a negative one, you are likely to continue to have negative thoughts for a while. You also tend to think about the past in the light of your current mood.

GMJ: So not being able to find a store clerk or getting called by a cranky phone rep can have a negative effect on a customer's behavior? Decisions can be based on perception, instead of reality?

Dr. Kahneman: Sometimes, yes. I mean, people should know that if they're in a bad mood, they're going to overestimate the likelihood of failure. People also should know that they're very prone to optimistic biases in judging how likely they are to succeed in different enterprises, and so on. People are wildly optimistic very often. And certain people exaggerate the impact of almost anything that they think about.

I have a "fortune cookie maxim" that I'm very proud of: Nothing in life is quite as important as you think it is while you are thinking about it. So, nothing will ever make you as happy as you think it will. Just thinking about things can make them seem very important.

GMJ: So how should people make reasonable decisions? Especially people like CEOs, who make decisions that affect a lot of people?

Dr. Kahneman: There are better and worse ways of making decisions. Probably the worst way is to look at the decision in isolation from everything else. If you are the CEO of a company, there are many categories of decisions that you make frequently. For those, you ought to have a policy. Then just apply the policy in a fairly standard and rigorous way rather than delving into each problem separately.

If you focus too much on each problem separately, you'll get very lost and make bad decisions. But when you get some distance from your problems and look at them as a category, class, or set of problems, you become more reasonable.

GMJ: So getting some context is key to avoiding errors in perception. But how do you know if your decision making isn't just an exercise in risk aversion? Or risk taking?

Dr. Kahneman: Well, there are many factors that determine whether people do or do not take risk. It is not correct to say that people avoid risks in general, because most people actually prefer some risks.

What *is* true about people is that they hate losing. They're much more sensitive to what they might lose than to what they might gain. So we say that people are loss-averse, not risk-averse. For example, you ask someone to toss a coin. If the coin shows tails, you lose $20. If it shows heads, you win X amount. And now I ask you, what would X have to be to make that gamble attractive to you? What people tend to say will be somewhere between $40 and $50. So people need to be compensated more than twice as much before a 50/50 gamble becomes attractive. I think that people evaluate gains and losses relative to some reference point and put more weight on the loss, not the gains.

GMJ: How do people figure out that reference point?

Dr. Kahneman: It depends on the person and the circumstances, but the anchoring effect is a characteristic error in judgment and decision making. Anchoring is a common effect when you are buying real estate. The asking price is an anchor. It's a number that sticks in your mind, and it's very difficult to get away from it. You don't think of the actual value of the house, you think of the price, then make all your decisions based on that. So recognizing that you're susceptible to anchoring is actually quite a useful thing. A lot of negotiations are about anchors.

GMJ: Speaking of which, explain to me why, when people do home remodeling, they tend to start out with a fairly reasonable budget, then more often than not they go over budget — and quite frequently they go . . .

Dr. Kahneman: Way over budget. One reason is that the same expense begins to look smaller in the context of the larger expense. My advice to people has always been that when you're buying an expensive house, buy the furniture at the same time. The amount that you will spend on the furniture will look small relative to the cost of the house. Otherwise, if you buy the house, and then stop, and then start buying the furniture, you'll buy furniture that isn't good enough for your house. That's because you begin to feel poor. So you actually should do everything at once; I think you make better decisions in doing everything at once. I mean, spending a thousand dollars seems like a lot of money, but the difference between $15,000 and $16,000 in remodeling your kitchen — that doesn't seem like a lot of money. So it's the same thousand dollars, but by embedding it in a larger amount, you've made it seem small.

GMJ: So context changes everything.

Dr. Kahneman: Everything.

THE FUTURE OF THE INTERNET

An interview with Internet co-creator Vinton Cerf
by Jennifer Robison

April 13, 2006

Most of the people who invented the great technologies — the telephone, the printing press, and the internal combustion engine, for example — that irrevocably altered the way humans live, work, and even think of humanity itself, share two common characteristics. The first is that they didn't know what they were getting us into back when they were toiling away on their world-altering advances. The second is that they're dead, which is inconvenient.

It's inconvenient because we will never know what they thought about when they were changing the course of humanity, why they did it, and what they wanted out of it — and that's a sad loss to history. In one way, Vinton Cerf, Ph.D., is like those other pioneers. Dr. Cerf, who designed the TCP/IP protocols and architecture of the Internet with pioneering computer scientist Robert Kahn, didn't recognize the impact of his work while he was doing it. But unlike them, and conveniently for us, he is very much alive — and kicking.

Most of us might decide that creating one world-altering contribution to humanity was enough, but Dr. Cerf has been at the forefront of several historic social changes. He led the team of MCI's advanced networking framework architects, which was key to getting individuals and businesses online. More recently Dr. Cerf joined the senior management team of Google, a company that may yet change the nature of business on the Internet, as well as the business model for all communications organizations. In the meantime, he's received dozens of awards, including the U.S. National Medal of Technology and the Presidential Medal of Freedom.

All of this gives Dr. Cerf a unique perspective on what is arguably the greatest advance of our age. In this interview, Dr. Cerf discusses the birth of the Internet, his thoughts on its future and its impact on how the world does business, and the social implications of his invention. But first, he explains why he'd like to lose his most famous title: "Father of the Internet."

Gallup Management Journal: You've been awarded countless honors, among them the title "Father of the Internet." Tell me how you invented the Internet.

Dr. Cerf: First of all, it would be wrong for people to solely attribute fatherhood of the Net to me. My involvement was very much in a collaborative mode, first with Bob Kahn, then later with many other people who participated in the further evolution of the Internet architecture. In fact, Robert Kahn, who is frequently recognized as another father of the Internet, started the project in late 1972 and early 1973 at the Defense Advanced Research Projects Agency. He invited me to work with him on this project in spring of 1973, when I was at Stanford. We had worked together on the ARPANET project [ARPANET was the first experiment in wide area packet switching] in 1969 and 1970, so I knew him. He realized that, when he was trying to figure out how to do this open network idea, he needed somebody who knew something about operating systems and how on earth to get this idea to work across a variety of different operating systems.

I happened to have been a graduate student at UCLA at the time when the first node of the ARPANET was installed at UCLA. My job was to write the software to interconnect a computer up to the ARPANET, and that's how I met Bob Kahn. Then four years later in 1973, when Bob was working on several other demonstrations of packet switching, the first one, the ARPANET, was very successful. So he started looking at packet switching in mobile radio and packet switching on satellite.

Now, you can understand the military interest here, because ships at sea have to communicate over radio, and satellite is particularly attractive because of its wide-area footprint. Mobile radio is needed in tactical communications. So if we were going to use computers in command and control, we needed to be able to incorporate this capability in ships at sea and in mechanized infantry.

So when Bob came out to Stanford in 1973, he was asking me how to get this packet satellite, packet radio, and ARPANET thing to work, how do we get all the networks to interconnect? *That* was the Internet problem. And that was what he and I basically solved during a very intense six months, from March to September 1973, and we came up with the basic design of the Internet architecture and the basic protocols.

So we wrote a paper together, which ultimately was published in May 1974 in the Communications of the Institute for Electrical and Electronic Engineering proceedings. That paper is now a classic, and copies of it have been auctioned off for as much as $4,800, much to my surprise. I don't have any more in my files; otherwise I'd be retiring by auctioning pieces of paper.

GMJ: In 1973, did you imagine anything like this? Did you ever think that this project you were working on would change human communication forever?

Dr. Cerf: Well, no. Our work in the early 1970s was all very technologically oriented; it was, "Can we do this? How can we do this? Can we show that it works? Can we standardize it? Can we make it an international standard?" And that occupied a good ten years before we got to the first rollout in 1983 and then another ten years to get to the point where the general public had access to it.

By 1989, however, I absolutely recognized the requirement to commercialize the Internet service. It was very clear by that time that it would not be possible for the government, either in the United States or elsewhere, to fund access to the Internet for the general public. And if I wanted that to happen, and by that time I did want everybody to have access to the Internet, it seemed to me the only way to do that was to build a business engine underneath it, which meant commercializing Internet service.

GMJ: How did commercialization of the Internet begin?

Dr. Cerf: Fortunately, the National Science Foundation, which at that time was sponsoring the NSF Net backbone, shared a common interest in pursuing that goal, so they took various steps that permitted commercialization to happen. They made it possible for the government-sponsored backbone to carry commercial traffic, which up until that time was not permitted. Then in 1992, Congress passed legislation that officially allowed that capability as the government carriage of commercial traffic. By 1995, the NSF Net backbone was retired because of the growth of the commercial service providers — the backbone service providers. So by 1989, I was very convinced that the Internet should be a commercial enterprise.

I don't think that I could possibly have envisaged all of the applications that have arisen on the network. It would be simply outrageous for me to make such a claim, and I don't. But it seemed to me that the standards were so open that it permitted just a huge range of experiments and trials to be conducted by very creative people who could find ways of using this network to exchange information and to supply services to interested parties.

GMJ: Do you think business is exploiting the Internet's full potential?

Dr. Cerf: Oh, not by any stretch. I mean, we're just barely scratching the surface of what we can do with this kind of communication technology. And I think you can see that almost daily as you look at new product announcements that involve networked devices. So I'm expecting to see many billions of devices using the Net to communicate with each other. This is not just for human communication, which has been tremendously valuable, or human sharing of knowledge, which has also been very valuable, but it can also be used for managing and controlling various devices.

So my entertainment system should be manageable through the network; third parties should be able to offer to me the ability to manage devices around the house and the office and in the car and maybe even on my person. Once these devices are able to communicate with each other, it means that third parties can build software that services those devices, interact with them, and manage them, or provide services to them.

You see this happening already as mobile phones become Internet-enabled and as you see more and more functionality being injected into personal digital assistants. I carry a BlackBerry with me — it's a mobile phone, and it's a PDA in the sense that it has calendar and e-mail. It also has access to the Net. And there have been times when the ability to do a Google search from a BlackBerry in some random spot has been extremely helpful — whether it's finding the nearest gas station or a restaurant or telephone number of the hotel that you're trying to get to, or even just exchanging e-mail with someone in order to coordinate where you're going. This kind of capability is very attractive. I think we are only at the beginning of understanding what we can do with communicating devices.

GMJ: That brings up a social point — it can be very difficult to unplug yourself. People call BlackBerries "crackberries" for a reason. Do you think electronic communication is supplanting face-to-face communication?

Dr. Cerf: No, I don't. There's a certain amount of rudeness that one can associate with BlackBerries or mobile phones or similar devices. I mean, sitting in a restaurant with someone and talking to someone else on a mobile phone is a kind of rudeness that we ought to resist. The same thing can be said about sitting there checking e-mail while you should be chatting with someone.

On the other hand, I have found my ability to stay in touch with a much larger number of people to be dramatically enhanced by having these capabilities. For one thing, they cross time zones, so that if I have an idea that I want to share with somebody, I don't have to wait. I just send them an e-mail and don't have to wait six hours because of the time difference. So I'm very attracted to e-mail in part for that reason and in part because it's a group communication medium in addition to a one-on-one medium. I can keep multiple people apprised of what's going on. The younger generation prefers instant messaging to e-mail; they think of e-mail as being old hat. Maybe when they get older, they won't feel that way, but right now the immediacy of interaction with their friends is very attractive. So I see this as simply enhancing social interaction as opposed to inhibiting it.

GMJ: But has it enhanced communication or only broadened it?

Dr. Cerf: In my view, all sorts of things have been enhanced by the convenient ability to communicate and to actually multitask. This is an interesting phenomenon. At Google, it's very common to have a meeting, and everybody brings their laptops, and while they're meeting, they're also doing their e-mail. Some have to be warned ahead of time that multitasking is a badge of honor as opposed to an insult and it's expected that you'll be able to do that. Kids are growing up now very accustomed to multitasking. If you walk into any teenager's room, you'll see a laptop going with a number of instant messaging windows open, a Google search happening, maybe they've got a television going in the background, and they've got their headset on listening to an MP3 that they downloaded. It's very common to see that kind of dynamic. So it's an expansion of the kinds of relationships that we're able to maintain.

GMJ: What do you think about wireless communications? Do you think that's going to make a huge change?

Dr. Cerf: I think it already has. You now see on the order of two billion mobiles in the wireless telephony world, and that has brought telecommunications to a cadre of users who never had access to telephony before or who had to wait years to get a wire line telephone. So in absolute numbers, it's made a huge difference. The expansion of functionality of these mobiles to include Internet applications is an even more powerful force, because it means that people are using wireless communications to get access to information that they never had before. So just on the pure telephony side, which is being augmented now by Internet access, that's important. Wireless access to the Internet has also had some interesting side effects — it's actually changed some of our behavior. We often leave a laptop at the dinner table and when questions come up that we don't have answers to, we Google it. And it allows for, in some sense, longer and more in-depth conversations to happen because otherwise we just get stuck — you know, who invented X or where is Y?

GMJ: It turns the Internet into our spare brain. And as such, do you think there's a danger to that?

Dr. Cerf: Perhaps. I do worry about how people do things if they don't memorize or can't remember things, because they are very dependent on being able to get access to them online. I am. I mean, I forget people's names now. And at the age of 62, I find my brain cells are starting to work more poorly than they did when I was 22, so I find myself turning to my e-mail in order to remember people's names. I'll do a Google desktop search because I know I was talking to some person about something. Now that's kind of embarrassing, but it suggests that Google is my solution to old age.

THE SUBPRIME MELTDOWN WILL BURN EVERYONE

An interview with Gallup Chief Economist Dennis Jacobe
by Jennifer Robison

June 14, 2007

The news about the U.S. subprime mortgage loan meltdown just keeps getting worse. The Center for Responsible Lending analyzed more than 6 million subprime mortgages issued from 1998 through the third quarter of 2006 and found that "2.2 million households in the subprime market either have lost their homes to foreclosure or hold subprime mortgages that will fail over the next several years." New Century Financial, the largest independent U.S. subprime mortgage lender, filed for bankruptcy, and 3,200 people — about half the company's workforce — lost their jobs. Numerous other subprime lenders have closed their doors, and others are sure to follow.

The Mortgage Bankers Association reports that the seasonally adjusted rate of loans entering the foreclosure process was at an all-time high in the last quarter of 2006, and "increases in delinquency and foreclosure rates were noticeably higher for subprime loans." And the National Association of Realtors reports that total existing home sales in April were 10.7% below those of a year ago, attributing the drop to the fact that many subprime loan products are no longer available.

But cheer up! The Dow continues to reach new record highs, far surpassing the 13,000 mark, right? And people who don't have a subprime loan or work for a subprime loan lender don't have any skin in the game, do they? Besides, the subprime debacle will be contained, won't it?

Federal Reserve Board Chairman Ben Bernanke believes the overall economy can withstand the problems in the subprime lending market, stating in a speech in Chicago, "The effect of the troubles in the subprime sector on the broader housing market will likely be limited, and we do not expect significant spillovers from the subprime market to the rest of the economy or to the financial system."

Not so fast, says Dennis Jacobe, Ph.D., Gallup's chief economist. The subprime crisis likely will affect everybody eventually. The reverberations will be subtle in some ways and overt in other ways. And it won't be over any time soon. In this interview, Dr. Jacobe discusses why the subprime loan market imploded, what effect this will have on credit and the economy, and whether you or your grandchildren will sell your house for more than you paid for it.

Gallup Management Journal: Subprime loans are generally made to people with poor credit histories. But there can't be all that many subprime borrowers. So why is there such a big ripple effect?

Dr. Jacobe: About 20% of the loans made last year were subprime. Probably another 20% to 30% involved creative refinancing, such as adjustable-rate loans that require borrowers to pay enough to cover the monthly payment for the first number of years, then the mortgage rate is scheduled to go up each year. Or they are "buy down" loans, which are the same kind of thing, but at a fixed rate: The first several years are at an artificially low rate, or you pay only the interest, but after a certain number of years you have a higher interest rate and/or balloon payment. So even if you don't have a subprime loan, problems in the subprime market will migrate to the creative financing market, and then to the regular prime mortgage market.

GMJ: How did the situation become a crisis so fast?

Dr. Jacobe: Most of these borrowers got subprime loans at high interest rates; it was the only opportunity they had to get a loan. And though some of these loans were clearly predatory, most of them were just expensive.

There will be a lot of debate about the difference, but when times are good, it's not easy for a regulator or a lender to say, "No, this is ill advised, and I'm not going to let you borrow money." Instead, what the lenders would say is, "Well, the value of the houses we're lending money on is increasing, so the real risk of making the loan is not high. If the borrower can't make the payments, they could sell or refinance the house and thus, avoid default." And when times were good, the booming housing market kept the default rate down.

But in the last year or so, housing prices in a lot of runaway markets have come down. Overall price levels and values have lowered. As a result, some of the people who have high-rate loans can't make their payments, and because they don't have any equity, they can't get out of their mortgage by selling the house. They often find they can't refinance for a number of possible reasons, such as the loan they would need to refinance might now exceed the value of the house, the new payments may exceed their ability to pay, their payment difficulties have further impaired their credit, or loan underwriting standards have tightened as loan defaults have increased. So the default rate goes up because of changing economic circumstances in general and declining housing values in particular.

GMJ: But this is predatory lending, isn't it?

Dr. Jacobe: Everybody is asking that — on Capitol Hill and everywhere else. Have lenders been taking advantage of people who don't know better? Were lenders getting borrowers into loans they couldn't pay, then putting them into foreclosure?

On the one hand, you can argue that providing mortgage loans for marginal borrowers is actually a good thing, because it gives these families a chance at homeownership that they might not get otherwise. Increasing homeownership is clearly a good thing.

On the other hand, making loans to marginal borrowers is usually done at higher interest rates and with the understanding on the lender's part that these borrowers are high risk and may default and lose their home. Of course, knowingly taking advantage of people by lending them money at very high rates with very high fees knowing they will be unable to pay it back can be seen as predatory lending.

In recent years, I think lenders and their regulators have tended to emphasize providing the home borrower with information and the attendant responsibility to decide for themselves whether they can make the loan payments the lender offers them. The idea is that more choices are obviously better than less for the potential borrower.

Personally, I tend to agree with the results of our recent Experian/Gallup Poll, which was completed in May. In that poll, only 16% of consumers told Gallup that they feel the availability of subprime loans is generally a good thing because more consumers can own a home, while 74% said it was a bad thing because borrowers get into loans they cannot afford.

I think the mortgage loan process is so complex that many borrowers tend to rely on their lender — and indirectly on banking regulators — to help them know how much they can borrow. Even more importantly, I think losing your home to foreclosure is such a terrible experience for the family and the community that lenders and regulators must accept some responsibility to help the consumer avoid predatory lending.

Now, the surge in home mortgage defaults has banking regulators taking more responsibility by forcing lenders to tighten their mortgage underwriting standards. As a result, there will be less mortgage financing available, not only because of the losses subprime lenders took, but also because of new regulatory sanctions.

GMJ: What effect will this have on the general housing market?

Dr. Jacobe: Well, it will affect home sales because all those marginal borrowers can't get into the market. So people who want to move up by selling either low-cost new homes or older homes can't sell their homes to these borrowers, because they can't get a loan anymore. When you take a significant percentage of the people who are buying homes out of the market, then home sales will go down. And when you add a significant number of foreclosures to that, you get so-called distress sales, which means that somebody just has to unload the house even if they take a loss. Or a lender takes it over in a bankruptcy filing and just wants to sell it, even at a loss. When that happens, it drives prices down some more. It is a cycle that builds until the market consolidates the excess inventory.

I agree with the 59% of consumers in our May poll who believe that the problems in the subprime market will spill over into the overall mortgage and housing markets, not the 25% who believe these problems will be contained.

GMJ: How long will that take?

Dr. Jacobe: Longer than many on Wall Street anticipate. I think what some people may have missed — because we haven't had a real, significant economic downturn in more than a decade — is that consumer finance in general has been flooded with liquidity for the last several years, the last four or five years in particular. So loan standards and lending standards that were established and maintained for many years were relaxed as lenders competed for borrowers. There was a lot of credit available, while the interest rates that the lenders paid for the money have been very low. So lenders could fund these loans and get good rates of return. The subprime market in particular was one of the few places you could get a really good rate of return. So the competition became intense, and lending standards declined as a result.

I think that many people associated with the mortgage and housing markets knew that there were excesses in the way loans were being underwritten and in housing prices. But just like any other kind of bubble, when you're looking at the current situation, you say, "My experience says this will burst, but right now I can't prove it, because the default rate's not bad and housing values are going up." So they stayed in and made more loans. And then the bubble burst.

Now, housing values will go back up, but the balance has to be addressed. Most of the speculators have gotten out of the market, and so, after some period of time, housing prices will rebound. History teaches us that. But there will be a period of consolidation, and prices will need to become more reasonable and less speculative. Unfortunately, this is a long process, usually measured in years, not months.

GMJ: What effect will this have on the economy in general?

Dr. Jacobe: There are at least three ways that it can have a general effect. One, the housing market itself has an impact on the economy overall. Many businesses are related to the housing market, such as home improvement, home furnishings, and appliance stores, as well as mortgage bankers and real estate brokers. A lot of those businesses, which have been booming, will suffer as a result of the downturn in the housing market.

Second, another part of the economy was driven by home equity loans. Some people got cheap loans based on the equity in their homes. Other people were using their homes as an ATM machine to support consumer spending — they could buy things that they might not have before, such as home improvements, cars, and boats — all kinds of things, because they took the equity out of their home and turned it into cash. People felt better about doing this because if the value of their house was going up, then they didn't worry as much about having more debt, and when interest rates were low, they felt like it was a good deal. But that also put many consumers deeper in debt.

The third thing that's going to happen as a result of the problems with subprime loans is that there can be a general effect on credit. I think that's the one problem that's hard to perceive right now, but I think it will happen. In general, we can expect banking regulators and the lenders they supervise to tighten consumer loan underwriting standards. That means there will be significantly less liquidity available to consumers than in the recent past. When that happens, generally speaking, consumers will tend to pull back [on spending] because they have less money available to them in terms of credit.

GMJ: Do you think all of this will cause the Fed to ease monetary policy? And if so, what will the upshot of that be?

Dr. Jacobe: Well, it depends on how much the current housing situation slows the economy. There's a lot of debate about this. My feeling is that the economy will continue to slow, and slow more than people anticipate, as we continue through this year. When I add in higher gas prices, then I think the economy can slow quite a bit more.

So, there will be a general economic effect, and I think it is likely to put us into a recession later this year or early next year. If it looks like we're going into a recession, then the Fed may cut interest rates. To some degree, that [action] depends on what's happening on the inflation front and in the world economy. If the world economy stays strong and the U.S. economy declines, as some people hypothesize it will, it's theoretically possible that the United States could continue to have inflationary pressures that will make the Fed feel uncomfortable about reducing interest rates. My own guess is that although the world economy has changed a great deal in recent years, I don't think it can continue to do well without the United States. And so I think if the U.S. economy goes into a significant slowdown or recession, then the world economy will slow, with some lag, and as a result, I think the Fed will cut interest rates late this year.

I also think we are likely to see a move in Congress to do something for subprime borrowers. In the Experian/Gallup Poll, we asked if the federal government should pass new legislation designed to help subprime borrowers keep their homes and avoid foreclosure; 57% said yes, while 37% said no. I think this legislation will happen because securitization — the process by which lenders sell mortgage loans to investors — has made it much more difficult for individual lenders to provide borrowers with any real degree of forbearance.

It used to be that most mortgage loans were made and held by local lenders. If the borrower got into trouble making their payments, then both the lender and the borrower had the ability and the incentive to find a way to help the borrower with some temporary relief that avoids foreclosure. Now, most mortgage loans are held by investors who have no contact with the borrower and no way to work with the borrower to prevent loan default and foreclosure. The current housing crisis will be the nation's first real experience with today's (securitized) mortgage finance system under distress. Evidently, the outcome of this test worries me a lot more than it does the Fed and the equity markets.

GMJ: *Given your far-from-rosy outlook, how do you explain the Dow's continued strength? Are you maybe too worried, while the economy might be a lot stronger than you think?*

Dr. Jacobe: That is always possible. Right now, however, I think the equity markets are being affected by all kinds of factors related to the world economy, globalization, and an abundance of liquidity worldwide. We see numerous mergers, companies buying back their stock, and other companies being taken private. In other words, I think there is a lot of money out chasing relatively fewer good investments.

I think the real thing that would hurt the equity markets and the economy is a credit crunch. It's theoretically possible that the excessive liquidity that's existed worldwide during the past several years could lead to a regulatory-induced credit crunch that could have all kinds of lenders pulling back. And if that happens, we'll have a problem of a totally different magnitude.

Whether and how you reconcile totally different underwriting perspectives by lenders and a reduced level of world liquidity with the current world economy may be a major issue during the months ahead. That's why many people who are watching the housing market (which I think is going to get a lot worse) think the stock market is a little too optimistic right now. On the other hand, maybe mortgage securitization and globalization have so changed things that the lessons of history no longer apply to the U.S. economy. We'll see.

GLOBAL MIGRATION PATTERNS AND JOB CREATION

by Jim Clifton, Chairman and CEO of Gallup

October 11, 2007

More and more often, global leaders are asking us the same simple, yet colossal, question: "Does anyone know for sure what the world is thinking?"

There is a great deal of classic economic data that record an infinite amount of human transactions, from GDP to unemployment to birth and death rates, that indicate what man and woman are doing. But there is no ongoing, infinite, systematic account of what man and woman are *thinking*.

Global leaders are right to wonder. To know what the whole world is thinking — not just what people in their own countries are thinking — on almost all issues all the time would certainly make their jobs a lot easier at the very least. At most, knowing what the world is thinking would create newfound precision in world leadership. Leaders wouldn't make mistakes and miss opportunities because they misjudge the hearts and minds of their constituencies and the other 6 billion with whom those constituencies interact.

We think we have found a very good answer to that very good question. We created a new body of behavioral economic data for world leaders that represents the opinions of all 6 billion inhabitants, reported by country and almost all demographics and sociographics imaginable.

We call it the World Poll. We've committed to doing it for 100 years.

The World Poll

We knew going in it was a monumental challenge, but creating the World Poll was even harder than we thought. To start, Gallup scientists combed the best public opinion archives, academic institutions, the United Nations, the World Bank, the European Union archives, the State Department, everything and everywhere we thought we might find existing information of this type.

We couldn't find it. There was no world poll. So we made one.

We knew the whole project hung on the questionnaire. It needed to cover almost every issue in the world, be translated accurately into dozens of languages, and be meaningful in every culture. Even more difficult was engineering consistent sampling frames in more than 100 countries from Ecuador to Rwanda, Iran, Russia, Afghanistan, Ireland, Cuba, Lebanon, Kazakhstan, Venezuela, Honduras, China . . . You get the picture.

Having constructed the questionnaire, our team of experts found its next biggest challenge was choosing a methodology to ensure consistent data collection so the whole set is comparable. For instance, when we ask about life satisfaction, everyone from a Manhattan socialite to a Masai mother has to be asked the same question every time in the same way with the same meaning and in their own languages so the answers could be statistically comparable. If the meaning of the questions isn't identical from language to language, culture to culture, year to year, the data are useless.

Furthermore, we needed to create the first-ever reliable and consistent benchmarks so leaders can see the trends and patterns. So we benchmarked wellbeing, war and peace, law and order, hopes and dreams, healthcare, suffering and striving, personal economics, poverty, environmental issues, workplaces, and on and on.

We have now completed the design, engineering, and first year of global data collection. The first-ever world poll on almost everything is done.

Then our Gallup scientists, affiliated academics, and colleagues from around the world who helped us make the poll got busy. They counted and sorted and used every known statistical technique to analyze exactly what the world is thinking. The conclusions are complex. This may be the great understatement in Gallup's history, but it's true.

For instance, when you dig deeply into the hopes, fears, motivations, and satisfactions of 1 billion Muslims, the more you learn, the more you realize how little the world knows, how wrong people are, and how much more complicated Muslim attitudes and opinions are than conventional wisdom would lead us to believe. Western leaders tell us religion drives Muslims to war. But Muslim extremists tell the World Poll that their anger is not about religion, it's about politics.

It's the same with the 3 billion people who live on $2 a day or less — the hungry half of the world's population. What they're thinking is very different from what most government agencies and NGOs understand and report. While we're rushing them food and medicine, most of them feel the only real solution is jobs.

Another example: One of the most important questions in the world is "What do Muslim women want?" Discovering what Muslim women want has been as big a surprise to us as anything we have ever seen. Muslim women want all the freedoms that their counterparts in the Western world have — they want the right to vote, to have the same rights that men do, and to hold leadership positions in government. The big surprise is that most Muslim men think Muslim women should have these too. And because women are half of the population, it's difficult to win in the new world unless they, their hopes and dreams, and their talents are integrated into the leadership of every organization, economy, and government in the world.

And those are just three demographics. Christians, Jews, Buddhists, old people, young people, black people, white people, communists, capitalists, Easterners, Westerners . . . These data are overwhelming because, while they offer answers to many questions that could never be answered before, they make us intensely aware of how little we know about what is in the hearts and minds of 6 billion people.

The great global goal

Gallup is committed to conducting the World Poll for 100 years, but we may have already found the single most searing, clarifying, helpful, world-altering fact. If used appropriately, it may change how every leader runs his or her country. But at the very least, it needs to be considered in every policy, every law, and every social initiative. All leaders — policy and law makers, presidents and prime ministers, parents, judges, priests, pastors, imams, teachers, managers, and CEOs — need to consider it every day in everything they do.

What the whole world wants is a good job.

That is one of the single biggest discoveries Gallup has ever made. It is as simple and as straightforward an explanation of the data as we can give. If you and I were walking down the street in Khartoum, Tehran, Berlin, Lima, Los Angeles, Baghdad, Kolkata, or Istanbul, we would discover that on most days, the single most dominant thought carried around in the heads of most people you and I see is "I want a good job." It is the new current state of mind, and it establishes our relationship with our city, our country, and the whole world around us.

Humans used to desire love, money, food, shelter, safety, and/or peace more than anything else. The last 25 years have changed us. Now we want to have a good job. This changes everything for world leaders. Everything they do — from waging war to building societies — will need to be done within the new context of the human need for a "good job."

How does this change everything?

- The leaders of countries and cities must make creating good jobs their No. 1 mission and primary purpose because securing good jobs is becoming the new currency for leadership. Everything leaders do must consider this new global state of mind, lest they put their cities and countries at risk.

- Leaders in education will be forced to think beyond core curricula and graduation rates. If you are a school superintendent or a university president, you'll need to recognize that students don't want to merely graduate — their education will need to result in a "good job."

- Lawmakers need to contemplate whether and how new laws attract or repel a wide range of individual value systems. If enough people are sufficiently repelled, then the new laws will effectively strangle job creation.

- Military leaders must consider it when waging war and planning for peace. They must ask themselves whether military strikes, occupations, or community policing will effectively build a growing economy with good jobs. The opportunity to have a good job is essential to changing a population's desperate, and violent, state of mind.

- The mayors and city fathers of every city, town, and village on Earth must realize that every decision they make should consider the impact, first and foremost, on good jobs.

The evolution of the *great global dream* is going to be the material of a million Ph.D. dissertations. But it's only the beginning of the story. The shift in importance to "a good job" leads to a significant change in the evolution of civilization. There are endless indicators, but the most evident change is in global migration patterns.

Man and woman probably appeared about 200,000 years ago on the savannah plains in what is now known as Ethiopia and fanned out across the Earth to improve their lives, their tribes, and their families. We have never stopped walking. The first to move have always been the boldest adventurers, explorers, and wanderers, and that's still true. Until rather recently in human evolution, the explorers were looking for new hunting grounds, cropland, territories, passageways, and natural resources. But now, the explorers are seeking something else.

Today's explorers migrate to the cities that are most likely to maximize innovation and entrepreneurial talents and skills. Wherever they can freely migrate is where the next economic empires will rise. San Francisco, Mumbai, and Dublin have become hotbeds of job creation. This phenomenon has occurred in other hot cities from Austin to Boston and Seoul to Singapore. Highly talented explorers with the best skills and the most knowledge are attracted to the best cities. When they choose your city, you attain the new Holy Grail of global leadership — brain gain.

Brain gain

Brain gain is defined as a city's or country's attraction of talented people whose exceptional gifts and knowledge create new business and new jobs and increase that city's or country's economy. To some degree, all cities of all sizes, everywhere in the world, have a success story of brain gain. Someone had a good idea, and its implementation created new jobs in that town. Brain gain is the big-bang theory of economic development. The challenge leaders face is how to trigger brain gain in their cities.

It's a new challenge, but an old issue. Twenty-five years ago, virtually every economist, liberal and conservative, forecast that the GDP of the United States would lose its first-place ranking and drop to third. News shows, newspapers, and business magazines predicted that Japan's GDP would be around $5 trillion, Germany's would be around $4 trillion, and the United States would fall to third at about $3.5 trillion by 2007.

The economists were partly right. Japan is at about $4.5 trillion, and Germany's at about $4 trillion too. But they couldn't have been more wrong about the United States. The country's GDP didn't fall. Over the last 25 years, it grew to $13 trillion. The best economists in the world were off by more than $10 trillion.

They were wrong because their economic models didn't include the most powerful variable of all: the migration patterns of the most talented people. Value is now created from piles of ideas and determination, not piles of materials and natural resources. The economists underestimated the massive force of innovation and entrepreneurship that led to a technology revolution.

Now global economists are saying that by 2040 or sooner, the U.S. GDP will fall to second, behind China. Their formulas assume that everything is linear or cyclical and that man is rational. China has more consumers and more low-wage producers, so logic dictates that China's economy will be an unstoppable juggernaut. That logic is likely to be just as colossally wrong this time because it doesn't consider where the next big build-out of innovation and entrepreneurship will occur. It doesn't consider brain gain or the migration patterns of talent. It could, however, be colossally right — but only if China becomes a center of innovation and enterprise, attracting and retaining highly talented people.

So, how many talented rainmakers would you need to change the GDP of one city and then one country?

Researchers counted how many people created the technology build-out that led to the $10 trillion of unplanned revenue growth over the last 25 years in the United States. It appears to be about 1,000 people. Just 1,000 unusual star innovators and rainmakers.

Some of those innovators, like Vinton Cerf, one of the founding fathers of the Internet, had a brilliant idea that others shared with the world. Some, like Meg Whitman, put together a brilliant team and business model that propelled the innovation. But if you only count the "stars," the key individual pioneers who initiated the single spark that ignited the breakthrough idea or company, you won't get much beyond 1,000. And of that 1,000, more than half were Americans who had migrated from other countries.

However, the inherent problem in looking for *only* the 1,000 Americans who created the unforecasted $10 trillion is that it overlooks too many lesser, but equally necessary, individuals — the great team members who supported the stars. Take Microsoft, for instance. We consider Bill Gates to be the poster child for this colossal economic engine, but Paul Allen, Steven Balmer, Jeff Raikes, and others played key roles. There would probably be no Microsoft if it hadn't been for them.

The same is true for all world-class economic achievements and small and medium-sized ones as well. There is a star inventor and/or enterpriser whom we credit with the innovation, but we often forget the innovator's good fortune to have had several stellar performers or Super Mentors in his or her universe.

Let me quickly review what exactly makes a star different from a typical, hardworking employee. A star creates large amounts of new human energy where none previously existed. That energy creates economic energy. The star's organization is the first and greatest beneficiary, but the organization sends the current out in the form of higher wages and more purchases. Its employees and suppliers earn more so they spend more money on things — cars and houses and computers, healthcare, movie tickets, groceries, and of course, taxes.

The energy weakens as it spreads, which is why Bill Gates hasn't made everyone in the world a millionaire, but the energy is nonetheless transmitted bit by bit throughout the star's organization, city, and country. The star's energy may be so strong it transmits all over the world. Proximity counts because the closer you are to the stars, the stronger the money currents are.

These enterprisers are not limited to business. One guy in a Midwestern U.S. city has built a $100,000,000 junior college from nothing, and it's thriving and growing. His great value to his city and the United States is not just creating educated workers for the labor force, but also in the creation of many new teaching, administrative, support, and technical jobs. Of course, he has also purchased and developed real estate, requiring the services and supplies of dozens and dozens of businesses of all types. This social entrepreneur has created $100,000,000 of energy out of nowhere. And his Midwestern city — and the rest of the country — is benefiting.

These stars juice their immediate economy and that of everything around them. They are drivers of GDP. Brain gain contributes to a country's GDP growth. A country grows one city at a time. A city grows one organization at a time. An organization grows one star at a time. And all organizations are economic engines for all cities.

But who are these stars? They could live almost anywhere. More often than not, they are single, young — between the ages of 25 and 35 — and have at least an undergraduate college degree. And most of them have not yet been discovered nor have they created their big invention or enterprise.

Therein lies the opportunity. If 1,000 world-class explorers and inventors were the heroes of the unforecasted $10 trillion, how many stars are there in the world? How many exceptional people should we be watching and tracking? How many are in your city, and what effect are they having on brain gain/brain drain? Because you want and need them all . . . the small, medium, and large stars.

The four types of stars
This math and interpolation are really rough approximations, but hopefully more precise than the calculations that mispredicted the U.S. GDP by $10 trillion.

If 1,000 individuals were the "Columbus-type" explorers who receive all the credit for the economic value they discovered and claimed, let's generously assume that they had 10 other world-class supporting cast members around them — 10 people who were so important that there would be no economic miracle without them. So that equals 10,000. We then multiplied the 10,000 builders of big businesses by 10 again to determine a rough gauge of how many inventors and rainmakers it takes to support the continuing growth of the total U.S. GDP. Ten thousand multiplied by 10 (to take into account and give credit to the dominance of jobs in small to medium-sized corporations, which make up about 70% of the U.S. workforce) equals 100,000. In other words, a mere 100,000 stars of varying sizes created the unforecasted current state of growth of the United States, a country of 300,000,000 people.

Here's the part that matters to leaders: These 100,000 stars would have created that growth wherever they resided. If they had all set up shop in Sioux Falls, Kansas City, and Fargo, it would have all happened in the American Midwest. If this group had all lived in Sao Paulo, Rio de Janeiro, or Brasilia, $10 trillion would have magically appeared in Brazil.

The math is simple. One star per $100 million of GDP growth.

If you were to ask how to significantly increase your city's GDP, we would say you need to find and develop 10 stars. And you should create the biggest incubator of talent possible. Your incubator is your energy and job pipeline for the future. It will take some time to see the outcomes you want, but you won't get them if you don't start with 10 stars. The only other alternative is to buy growth, like companies do, with acquisitions. Corporate leaders face the organic vs. acquisition growth issue all the time, and they know that organic growth is the best long-term strategy for any organization or community of people.

To get a better idea of how to identify and incubate the stars, our team coded the characteristics of several hundred extraordinarily successful business, political, and nonprofit leaders. Only four categories or codes were needed to classify them all.

1) Innovators

Innovators get ideas that create new products, new markets, stock value, and hatch thousands of jobs.

They are often struck with their discovery while employed by an organization — a hospital, the government, a corporation — or most often during their university studies. They are as likely, however, to follow through on their discovery outside that organization as within it. In any case, the discovery creates the next big surge of energy for increased economic activity and subsequent job hatching.

What makes Innovators stars isn't just their creative capacity, but also their rare talent to seek innovation in all aspects of their lives. Brilliant ideas are often born from seeking solutions to difficult problems, and

Innovators are able to solve the problems and realize the idea. However, they aren't necessarily the ones who bring it to market.

2) Entrepreneurs

Entrepreneurs are most recognizable as super-salespeople or rainmakers. Entrepreneurs are those who see an idea, recognize the potential, figure out the necessary steps for making the idea a reality, and then bring the Innovator together with supporters to form a new venture. Entrepreneurs bet their money or career on a new idea, whether it's a new business or a new initiative within an organization. Entrepreneurs have the rare gifts of optimism and determination, which are, and probably will remain, the new most valuable resources in the world. Optimism and determination are more valuable in the equation than creativity and innovation because they are rarer.

It's important also to recognize "social entrepreneurs" in this category, as they are just as crucial to building hot, growing cities. Social entrepreneurs provide surges of positive energy through philanthropies. The work these entrepreneurs do enhances the culture of their city and always increases the wellbeing of their communities. These social enterprisers not only create better cities, their organizations are economic engines and job-hatching machines.

3) Superstars

Superstars are extremely rare creative achievers, people unusually gifted in the arts, entertainment, or sports. They're famous authors, singers and other musicians, artists, chefs, architects, actors, fashion designers, politicians, soccer and basketball players, etc. Such celebrities need their own category because they are valuable magnets for the cities where they live and work, but mostly because they're economic engines themselves. They create huge new amounts of economic energy from their movies, books, concerts, sports championships — the things they do, the related businesses that promote them, the causes they support, and on and on.

4) Super Mentors

Innovators, Entrepreneurs, and Superstars rely, whether they know it or not, on genius developers. We call such developers Super Mentors. They are the people who say, "Your idea could become a company. I'll line up investors for you." Or, "We need to get behind that professor's idea. He needs a lab here in town." Or, "Let's start a youth program that's the best in the country."

There are several varieties of Super Mentors. Often they are "city fathers," rich businesspeople who care deeply about their city. They can be great college presidents or the heads of philanthropies or religious leaders or CEOs. Sometimes they're just average citizens with a deep commitment to the place where they live and the ability to find and encourage raw talent. In any case, Super Mentors have a gift for identifying and developing young stars and strong hands to guide and lead them.

Super Mentors also have the rare capacity to command broad support and participation in local initiatives that otherwise wouldn't happen. The best and fastest growing cities in the world have an informal, never-elected group of Super Mentors. They work outside the local government and meet regularly to determine activities and strategies to help their city and people win.

One could argue that this group of Super Mentors makes a bigger and more positive impact on cities than do local governments. They have as much or more access to money and influence within the community as government leaders do, and they have the great advantage of speed and fewer barriers. And they serve a critical function — they are the very kindling that starts the fires of Innovators and Entrepreneurs.

Creating brain gain

Talented people create brain gain. Brain gain and brain drain are among the most crucial factors for the growth and wellbeing of any organization — from a one-employee business to the most powerful government on Earth. The most important issue for leaders is to identify and cultivate the conditions that create brain gain. They have to know the key factors.

We ask 100 core questions in our standard World Poll survey regarding seven critical conditions of life — conditions that are present in every country. When any of these conditions are higher or have momentum, it is likely that brain gain and GDP are higher. The seven critical conditions cover law and order, food and shelter, work, economics, health, wellbeing, and citizen engagement. There are several question items per each condition. For instance, "Do you feel safe walking alone at night in your community?" is one of four questions that measure the human condition of law and order. At the other end of the behavioral economic algorithm is "Have you volunteered your time to an organization . . ." which factors into the condition of citizen engagement.

Each domain is never static; things are always getting a little better or a little worse. Because they are not static, they can't be "resolved" — cities and countries must improve them continuously. Furthermore, we found that there is an order of importance to the issues, and that the higher the scores on these issues, the greater the potential for higher brain gain and GDP. A leader's biggest challenge is creating momentum on any of these critical domains.

Law and Order. The presence of law and order is the first and most important manageable condition. Take Sierra Leone, for instance. Nearly half of Sierra Leoneans say they have had money stolen in the past year, and nearly 3 in 10 say they have been mugged or beaten. These figures are among the highest we've found so far. Without law and order, Sierra Leoneans will be severely hindered as they rebuild their country after a violent, decade-long civil war. When law and order improves in Sierra Leone, so will GDP and life expectancy — currently age 40.

Food and Shelter. This is the same basic need Abraham Maslow identified 50 years ago. But as important as it is, we found it to be No. 2 on the new scale of wellbeing — as we saw in the "law and order" example, one's ability to obtain food and shelter may depend on law and order and is also highly related to life expectancy in lower income countries. In the United States, 10% say there have been times when they haven't had enough money to provide adequate shelter for their families in the past year, and 17% say they didn't have enough money for food. Those numbers are 36% and 27% in Russia. Consider the difference in each country's GDP. But in both cases, if this condition improves, brain gain and GDP will increase.

Work. As Freud said, "Love and work are the cornerstones of our humanness." Work is crucial to every adult human because work holds within it the soul of the relationship of one citizen to one government and one country. The most important World Poll discovery, so far, is that the primary driver of almost everyone is a "good job." This particular condition relates to net migration in high-income countries and GDP growth in low-income countries, but it is also a core influence of elections, revolution, and war.

While food and shelter and law and order are basic needs and are associated with self-preservation, work is where wellbeing turns the corner. This is where positive emotions that lead to creativity and openness are built. Good work facilitates a higher standard of living, higher potential for health, and higher wellbeing.

Economics. When perceptions of economic confidence have positive or negative momentum, it may potentially affect local economics and GDP. If an Innovator doubts the vitality of his personal, local, or national economic situation, he'll believe that Super Mentors won't come to his aid, or that the government restrictions are too onerous, or that his customer base is too narrow and always will be, and he'll never implement the idea. And a potential star fades, as does a potential spike in the GDP.

Health. This condition tracks specific health problems. We ask the whole world "Do you have health problems that prevent you from doing any of the things people your age normally can do?" Condition-specific questions range from the presence of physical pain and sleeplessness to whether one smokes and exercises and satisfaction with personal health.

Health highly correlates to wellbeing in low-income and middle-income countries. Healthy people create more vibrant communities and more productive workplaces, which contribute to productivity, brain gain, and quality GDP growth.

Wellbeing. While the health domain reports perceived physical and mental health, wellbeing reports the presence of suffering or thriving, misery or inspiration, feeling controlled or feeling independent. This is a crucial metric because all good things happen in the presence of high wellbeing. Many world leaders argue that the ultimate act of leadership is to improve gross wellbeing (GWB) versus increasing gross domestic product (GDP). Maybe. In any case, this "soft" issue affects a population's ability to innovate, improve, and invent, because it reports the all-important presence of hope.

Engaged Citizens. Citizen engagement is the actualization of real global altruism. This is the domain of world-class social entrepreneurs. It is the ultimate act of all leaders of all ranks because this is how leadership touches absolutely every constituency in the community.

Citizen engagement is the Mother Teresa domain of the World Path because it explains charitable giving not only of money, but also of time, and willingness to help strangers in need. It's the most precious and sophisticated value, and it speaks to the genius of Super Mentors. And it has the biggest potential returns of all for brain gain and subsequent GDP, especially in higher income countries.

Citizen engagement creates two kinds of magic. It generates new multiples of relationships between wide ranges of citizens, which breeds cooperation, productivity, citizenship, and patriotism. Positivity about one's country, and more particularly, one's community, creates an environment that makes talented people want to come and stay.

Leadership

From the very beginning of our 70 years of observing and studying the practice of leadership, we've known that unless a city or country has several committed, admired, and talented leaders in place, growth won't occur.

The Gallup Path behavioral economic model for societies assumes that the primary purpose of all "new world" leadership is to create an environment in which talented people want to live and work. This new global leadership responsibility rises above every other duty. Attracting, retaining, and developing talent in your organization, city, and country is now a more important variable than natural resources, ports, and even direct investment.

An effective global leader must see the task not as "fixing the problem" because brain-drain problems are almost always too complex to quickly fix. Rather, leaders must get the solution headed in the right direction. The job of leaders is to use strong hands to yank their organizations, their cities, and their countries onto the right path.

A successful team of global leaders will need both state-of-the-art classic economics, such as GDP, inflation, population, and birth rates and state-of-the-art behavioral economics, such as law and order, citizen engagement, and wellbeing to affect the migration patterns of the most talented people and create the next global economic empire.

SMALL COMPANIES, BIG RESULTS IN MEXICO

by Jennifer Robison

March 13, 2008

The state of Puebla in south central Mexico might be the last place one would look for high-powered, sophisticated management science. Most of the businesses in Puebla are small. The state seems thousands of miles away from the cutting-edge companies of the global economy. And many people outside the region probably haven't heard of Puebla, Mexico.

But don't let Puebla's obscurity fool you. The state has become the locus of some small but remarkable businesses using the same science as the biggest and best companies in the world. And those businesses are getting powerful results.

PUEBLA, MEXICO

Though it may be surprising to find small companies — or PyMEs, the Spanish acronym for small and medium-sized enterprises (pronounced "pea-mays" in English) — in remote venues using the same science in the same way to the same effect as does, say, Toyota, it's no accident. It's the result of the Puebla Job Creation Laboratory, a joint project of the government of the state of Puebla and Gallup.

In 2005, Mario Marín Torres, the governor of the state of Puebla, asked Gallup to help him fulfill some of his campaign promises: reduce poverty throughout the state, increase Puebla's domestic and international competitiveness, develop global best practices to bring world-class investment and technology to the state, and establish Puebla as a globally recognized center for management technology and productivity that can be linked to organic job creation. To help him in this endeavor, Governor Marín appointed his secretary of labor and competitivity, Jose Antonio Lopez Malo, to work with Gallup to convert promises to reality.

It was a tall order. Gallup needed to create what is, in essence, an education, job creation, and intervention program for small to medium-sized enterprises.

But it was a smart plan for several reasons. Globalization has brought competition to areas of the world that previously felt safe from it. These days, Mexican manufacturers are worried about competitors in China, who are worried about rivals in Southeast Asia, who may someday soon lose business in places that can provide even lower manufacturing or labor costs. Also, most Mexicans — in fact, most workers everywhere — work for companies of fewer than 500 people. In Mexico, small businesses provide 71% of formal employment and about 50% of the GDP.

What's more, Gallup research has revealed that in countries around the world, what people want is a good job. One of the best ways to create sustainable jobs is through organic growth. Unlike growth that comes through purchases of other companies (think of the GE model), "organic growth" occurs when a company creates more transactions with its current customer base and with continuously growing margins. Low-cost loans, business development plans, and small business training programs and the like are all necessary, but good management is the true accelerant that can turn struggling businesses into flourishing ones.

And that's what Governor Marín wanted Gallup to do for the state of Puebla — provide the fuel for individual businesses to grow so that they could create the jobs that spur economic development.

No magic number

As mentioned before, this science will work in any good company regardless of size. But that doesn't mean the science can be inserted on a whim. For Governor Marín's plan to work, the science had to be carefully adapted and administered to the PyMEs in a way that provided them with the best chance for measurable success. Because there is not an infinite number of Gallup management experts in Puebla, and because every participating PyME would require a considerable amount of input from a consultant, the number of companies invited to participate in the first cohort was deliberately kept small — only 32.

Those businesses, however, represent the local economy rather well. Some are tiny, with only a handful of employees who serve a very narrow market. Some are well on their way to becoming large companies but facing tough challenges. As Patricio Zorilla, the president of Ultravision — a radio, pay television, and Internet access company with about 300 employees — put it, "We're a small company, and we have a good product. But we need to work very fast and very efficiently if we want to get bigger or even to compete with the really big guys in communications." Each company, however, was exceptionally well-run and well-managed.

Delivery

Roberto Rojas, Ph.D., led the design and deployment of the PyME Growth and Job Creation Project. He faced special challenges from the project's beginning.

"We couldn't just walk into companies and tell them what to do," Rojas says. "They know their businesses better than we ever could. But we know the science. We had to deliver it in the way that would be most beneficial to them." And he had to figure out how to deliver it quickly, efficiently, and in a way that would create measurable success as determined by company growth, employee engagement, and job creation throughout each company.

Because a full-scale intervention in each business was impossible, Rojas concentrated on influencing high-level management strategy in each company. Once a month for five months, the executives came to the Gallup office for in-depth workshops. But before they even began, the executives were introduced to the program Rojas and his team had created — the "Impact Plan Plus." In essence, the Impact Plan

Plus integrated three basic components: creation of a shared vision for growth, development of strengths-based leadership, and increased employee engagement levels.

To create the vision for growth, the plan introduced executives to Gallup's Business Growth Strategies 13 (BG[13]) — 13 concepts such as customer engagement, core competencies, and regional and global growth opportunities that, while not directly actionable, gave the leaders the food for thought that companies grow on. Then the PyME executives took the Clifton StrengthsFinder, an assessment designed to measure the presence of key talents — patterns of thought, feeling, and behavior that can be productively applied. Next, they were coached on how they could best build on their individual talents to develop leadership strengths.

Finally, Rojas and his team explained employee engagement and the role it plays in creating productivity, sustainability, and profit growth. They also outlined how the Q^{12}, Gallup's 12-item employee engagement survey, would be administered in their companies — and what they should to do with the results.

"We went to see what Gallup had to offer, and we immediately thought that this is what we needed," says Ramon Gamero, human resources director of the 16-store home improvement chain Tudogar. "The Q^{12} in general was interesting because we realized our employees are really engaged with their work, but we have to do more with talents. This we learned right away."

The executives were introduced to the Clifton StrengthsFinder early because they needed to know their talents to use them to build leadership strengths. They also needed to understand strengths philosophy and language so they could explain and apply it throughout their organizations. And the executives from the PyMEs were anxious to learn.

"We were very interested in the program, because we have full field ISO 9000 certification. We were interested in learning how to use Gallup's program as a tool to help us meet those standards and to engage employees to ensure the continuous growth of our quality systems," says Esmeralda Garcia, quality manager for IVI Construction. The firm employs 90 managers as well as technical and office staff and, depending on the season and market, up to 900 people who build housing for low-income families in and near Puebla City. "But very, very specifically and most importantly, we wanted to learn about talents and how through these talents you could engage your employees."

To help make "using talents to engage employees" a simpler process, Gallup created a talent "map" for each company — a visual that showed the variety of talents that were found in their management ranks. "We analyzed the talent map in depth," says Gamero, "and with the Four Keys [to Great Management, a coaching and analysis method that helps individual managers work with their reports' strengths, limitations, styles, and needs] assessment, we have a whole lot of information for decision making and improving [our] teams."

Getting started

To start creating the Impact Plan Plus, two Gallup management experts conducted site visits. This was a crucial component of the program. The consultants had to know the businesses well to make actionable suggestions, and the executives had to believe that the consultants knew enough to know what they were talking about.

Based on what the Gallup consultants learned from the site visits, they identified key stumbling blocks for growth at each PyME, presented them to company executives, then worked with the executives to create their Impact Plan Plus. That's when they started talking about the BG[13] in depth.

"We were working from the inside out," says Rojas. "We put growth at the center of this framework. You may think that this is all very obvious, but it isn't obvious if you don't give direct thought to these issues. We very much wanted each company to be successful, but for that to happen, they had to define what success means within their company."

At the same time, Gallup worked with each company to analyze its structure. The resulting organizational map was key not only to the Q^{12} implementation, but also to helping each business understand how employee engagement played out across the company. The employee engagement consulting and analysis was accomplished in a single month.

Thus, by the third month of the PyME project, executives of each company were awash in new management intelligence. They had received training in strengths development, employee engagement, management science, and strategic planning — and were then sent back to their companies to implement it.

"The impact plan was very helpful to us because we're coming from the hard side of construction," says Garcia. "We're more process oriented [on] the hard, cold side of the industry. When we discovered that you can use your talents deliberately and efficiently and what specifically you can do to engage your employees, we realized that this is another very important side of the organization that complements the one we have already succeeded with. It gave us a comprehensive solution for dealing with a very important human factor."

Implementation

Each company implemented its learning in ways that best suited its culture. At Ultravision, Zorilla made what he learned part of the company's everyday culture and put one person in charge of the employee engagement and strengths implementation. "The studies and learning and all the measurement tools showed us that we needed to [make] some changes, so we did — and we're still doing it," Zorilla says. "It's part of [our] everyday work to [manage] this way."

Garcia and her team of engineers and construction workers found the "soft side" of management a bit hard to swallow at first, but they understand productivity in a very concrete way. So they made the implementation process-oriented. First, they started matching organizational needs with individual talents. Then they paired engagement problems, as identified by the company's Q^{12} employee engagement results, with specific action plans to combat them.

Next, they tackled company-specific issues, such as quality, with what they learned in their management training. And they got very, very serious about managing individuals. "Through what we learned in the intervention, we've classified the employees based on performance — A, B, and C employees," says Garcia. "We decided to work hard with the A and B employees and leave the C, where the attrition occurs mainly."

In the fourth month of the program, Gallup assessed each business' progress and provided formal and informal mentoring and support on leadership talents and business challenges. Some companies were able to integrate the new management approaches and science into their organization more quickly than others, but almost all of them could benefit from some degree of mentoring and support. So, whenever a business leader had a problem or a question or needed advice, his or her coach was on the phone or at the site with a suggestion.

The fifth month brought a final review and another round of formal coaching. This was the last month of the program, when everything came together. Though five months seems an extremely short period to absorb this much new information and learning, much less put it to work, each PyME had to show measurable performance improvements to demonstrate the value of the program.

Change up

Some PyMEs showed more improvement than others. But the improvements that several of them showed are remarkable, especially considering the time frame and learning curve. Overall turnover at Tudogar dropped from 90% to 40% after the company implemented its focus on employee engagement and strengths-based approach to employee development. The company has also increased the number of training seminars that managers scheduled with employees from 58 a year to 223 in six months.

The program boosted Ultravision's growth plans and prepared it for rapid changes. Ultravision has gotten so big so fast that "sometimes it starts to get a little bit messy," as Zorilla said. But since the intervention, he's found it easier to put the right people in the right jobs. "I really like talent-based structure because it is very operational. I invested money in doing this because I hoped that it could help our teams feel more like part of the company and feel responsible. We needed this to compete with the big monsters of telecommunications and to grow 25% a year, which is the industry standard."

IVI Construction is also facing rapid growth — the company has built 4,468 houses since it was founded in 2000, and its goal for this year is to complete the building of 1,370 homes. Garcia believes that what they've learned through the program has ameliorated some of the negative aspects of fast expansion. "In terms of sales, [we've] been growing, but that is not necessarily a consequence of the Gallup program. It's because we are good at selling," says Garcia. "On the other hand, what we've learned has helped reduce attrition, and we've created 15 new positions."

These tools

So the governor of Puebla, the managing director of Gallup Puebla, and the PyME business leaders were all right — you *can* jump-start growth with just the right application of management science. Rojas' Impact Plan Plus has become part of each PyME's DNA, and it will be continued, even without Gallup's direct involvement.

But that's not all these successful businesses want. Every one of them wants to broaden the scope of what they've learned, having seen what this learning has done for top management. As Gamero says, "The tools — the Q^{12}, the StrengthsFinder, and the Four Keys — are very important, and now we consider [them] as essential for solid growth. We want to continue this implementation throughout the company. We should all have these tools."

NEWS FLASH: MONEY DOES BUY HAPPINESS

An interview with economist Angus Deaton
by Jennifer Robison

April 10, 2008

Money won't buy you love, you can't take it with you, and loving it is the root of all evil — or so the sayings go. But some heavy-hitting international economic research indicates that money *can* buy happiness, or at least a more valued life. So says Angus Deaton, Ph.D., the Dwight D. Eisenhower Professor of International Affairs and Professor of Economics and International Affairs at the Woodrow Wilson School of Public and International Affairs and the Economics Department at Princeton University. Though Dr. Deaton's research focuses on the areas of health, economic development, household behavior, and poverty around the world, he knows a lot about happiness. And he doesn't necessarily approve of it.

It's not that Dr. Deaton doesn't like happiness or believe that people shouldn't be happy; rather, he believes that happiness is not the healthiest goal a society can have — or perhaps the highest good to which it can aspire. In this provocative conversation, Dr. Deaton explores whether life satisfaction or happiness measures are important or meaningful and whether the pursuit of happiness or wealth matters more to societies than the development of human potential. He also discusses why foreign aid — both social and financial — to emerging countries might do more harm than good.

Gallup Management Journal: Let's start with the big thing: life satisfaction. Is that the same thing as happiness?

Dr. Deaton: That's a big can of worms. The psychologists who investigate these things often think that they get pretty much the same answers when they ask about your life satisfaction as when they ask how happy you are. There's somewhat of an industry trying to figure out what exactly people have in their heads when they answer those questions.

For me, I like to treat the question as just what it says, which is to evaluate your life. The Gallup World Poll also asks questions about enjoyment, and about laughing and smiling, which correspond more closely to what we usually think of as happiness. And it turns out that those are not always the same as life satisfaction, though there is a good deal of overlap. But happiness and life satisfaction are not the same. So let's use satisfaction from now on, but if we think of it as happiness, we will be in good company.

GMJ: That simplifies things. Now to make them complex: How is income related to life satisfaction or happiness?

Dr. Deaton: I hope the work I've been doing will change the way people think about that. There's a lot that we just don't understand [about how income relates to satisfaction or to happiness], but the first thing to realize is that they seem to be strongly positively related to one another.

Richer people seem to be happier, or at least they say they're more satisfied with their life, which is what you might expect. We all struggle to get richer, and we hope it will make us happier. That doesn't mean it necessarily will. But the belief in much of the literature is that as countries get richer over time, their populations don't actually get any more satisfied with their lives.

GMJ: Is there a point at which income no longer affects life satisfaction? It's said that after the first $10 million or so, money is just a way of keeping score.

Dr. Deaton: I don't think we have much data on the Bill Gateses of this world. One view is that income only really matters when you're really poor. In Sierra Leone, a quarter of all children die before they're five years old. People don't have enough to eat a lot of the time. You would think that because their basic needs are not being met, and they have horrible diseases and worse, a little money surely must make them happier. And that seems to be true.

Some people have argued that once you get beyond that point, once such horrible things aren't happening to you, money doesn't really matter anymore. And that's being claimed by a number of writers, mostly on the grounds that the argument seems plausible, and there's been some evidence for it.

GMJ: *But your work suggests that's not true.*

Dr. Deaton: That's right. I'm not the first person to show, and the Gallup data is particularly clear, that richer countries are not only more satisfied than poor countries, but also more satisfied than somewhat less rich countries. The United States is richer than Greece, and it's also more satisfied than Greece. And Greece and the United States are more satisfied than Chad or Sierra Leone or Mali.

GMJ: *What can a happy society accomplish that a less happy one can't?*

Dr. Deaton: That's a really good question. Maybe nothing. One of the things I'm really interested in is, are these life satisfaction or happiness measures important? Should we care about them? I'm not at all sure that we should.

GMJ: *That seems contrary to the Declaration of Independence, which claims for Americans the right to the pursuit of happiness.*

Dr. Deaton: I grew up in Scotland with a Calvinist upbringing. We were brought up to believe that happiness is a bit wicked. I'm probably trying to discount a cultural prejudice — you know, I think of happiness as a sort of Timothy Leary taking LSD kind of thing that's probably bad for you. But on a concrete level, I'm very interested in economic development around the world.

So why is it important for Indians or Chadians to get richer? Why do we care about that stuff? Why not just leave them be? I think one of the answers is that happiness is not what really matters; what really matters are people's capabilities and the opportunities that they have before them.

For example, if a mathematical genius or a Mozart dies of some horrible infection in Africa at age five, we've all lost something important. Sometimes, circumstances prevent it from happening. For example, one of the top orthopedic surgeons in New York City is a Ghanaian who was brought in malnourished to a mission hospital in Ghana, and now as a surgeon, he can do things that no one else can do.

If we get these countries so the people in them have more money and their health is better, I'm not sure I really care whether the people are happier or not. It's their ability to function that really matters. Do you see my point?

GMJ: Your point is that the vital thing is the ability to live a good life.

Dr. Deaton: Yes, and people can be taught to be happy with and accept things that really aren't very good for them at all, so that happiness, even life satisfaction, is not a very reliable guide. For generations, women accepted a subservient position. I don't think that's a very good thing. And if you'd asked the women then, many of them would have said they were happy with this position. There's the sense that what people tell you about their life satisfaction is not necessarily a very good measure in some circumstances.

GMJ: If you start every morning with a bottle of whiskey and a slice of chocolate cake, you might be pretty happy all day too. But you won't necessarily accomplish anything.

Dr. Deaton: That's it. That's what I believe. And the work I did on the Gallup World Poll was partly to see whether life satisfaction measures lined up with the more familiar measures of the quality of people's lives, such as their income, their health, and their political and civil rights. If you look across countries, they line up pretty well in the income dimension — people in rich countries seem to be more satisfied with their lives. And they line up pretty well in the political dimension too. What's happened in Eastern Europe and the former Soviet Union seems to have made people very unhappy, and that seems perfectly reasonable to me.

But the bit that doesn't line up is health. One of the worst epidemics in history, HIV/AIDS, is ravaging Africa, and it doesn't seem to have any effect on people's life satisfaction. So if you think life satisfaction is all there is to life, then we shouldn't worry about AIDS in Africa because it's not making Africans very unhappy. To me, that is an unacceptable position.

GMJ: Considering what you know of health, life expectancy, and life satisfaction, what should donors or wealthy countries focus their philanthropy on? Building economies in poor countries or healthcare? Infrastructure or education?

Dr. Deaton: All of those things. Good health, good education, democracy, the ability to purchase goods are all elements of a good life and are important in their own right. It's quite hard to measure them and say which one is most important at any given time. That's supposedly what the political process is about. But I'm not one of the people who believes that you can bypass the need to keep tabs on each of those things by saying as long as people are happy, or satisfied with their lives, then we don't have to worry about those things in and of themselves. Again, people seem to be quite satisfied with their lives even in really bad situations, such as the AIDS epidemic.

The other part is that I believe that the ability to participate in society, having enough purchasing power, and being healthy are important. Health is fundamental. If you're dead, most things that might make you happy are not worth very much, if you know what I mean. And if you're not healthy, it's very hard to earn a decent income. So having income helps you maintain your health, and having health helps you maintain your income. Education is exactly the same sort of thing — it helps you earn, but it brings you lifelong benefits other than earning.

GMJ: Dr. Deaton, do you see any way of ending poverty in places like Mali?

Dr. Deaton: Well, yes and no. But remember, I'm not very sure about this, so I don't want to suggest this is something research has established. But all countries were once as poor as Mali, right? All of the rich countries today were really poor once upon a time. When I was born in Edinburgh in 1945, the infant mortality rate there was higher than it is in India today. Now India is not Mali, but improvements can sometimes happen remarkably quickly. That's not controversial, but it's worth keeping in mind. The harder thing, and I think this probably underlies your question, is what can *we* do to eliminate poverty in Africa? And I'm not convinced that there's very much that we can do, actually.

That's the bit that's controversial, and I don't know that that's true, but I'm skeptical that much can be done from the outside. The obvious thing to do to relieve poverty [in a given country] is pour money into it, but if the government of the country has little interest in reducing the poverty of its people, you may not be able to do much good that way. The aid money might be diverted to Swiss bank accounts, or food aid could be used by warlords as a weapon to keep their troops fed and prolong a war. The literature from many of the more thoughtful NGO workers who have been on the front lines is often very bitter and skeptical. Even the humanitarian aid process has terrible problems, let alone the attempt to make economies grow by lending money at discounted interest rates.

GMJ: And yet we're morally obligated to do something.

Dr. Deaton: Well, there's the Hippocratic oath. You might say that we're morally obligated not to do any harm. And you could argue that attempts to pump money into those countries actually end up doing harm. In Africa, the amount of money readily available to the government is typically very small, and much of it comes from foreign aid. There's very little effort put toward developing domestic talent, so if we pour in money, what talent countries have is going to be distracted by fighting for the aid instead of doing things to develop the country. So when you say, "We have to do something," and that something involves giving money, you might actually be doing harm.

GMJ: Bono doesn't want to hear that.

Dr. Deaton: No. He certainly doesn't want to hear that. He's been told often enough, but he won't have anything to do with it. Nor Bill Gates. He's a much more serious figure in this. And there is no doubt good work being done.

GMJ: So how should one help? What can businesses do?

Dr. Deaton: One thing I'm sure that we can help with is basic science. For instance, if we were to figure out a vaccine for malaria or figure out what causes HIV/AIDS, it would be a huge gift to Africa. And individuals can do little things. Helping a village build a school, that sort of thing, I think that's probably right.

I think trouble comes from larger scale activities that bring all the bad guys in. Also, those things don't work, and businesspeople do like to see results, don't they?

WHY GLOBALIZATION IS OVERRATED

An interview with economist John F. Helliwell
by Jennifer Robison

September 11, 2008

John F. Helliwell, Ph.D., is one of the world's most prominent economists. In this interview, he offers the types of insights into macroeconomics for which he is renowned — and his observations refute just about everything we think we know about globalization.

Dr. Helliwell, the Arthur J.E. Child Foundation Fellow of the Canadian Institute for Advanced Research and Professor Emeritus of Economics at the University of British Columbia, has taken an extremely close look at globalization. As he discusses here, much of globalization's reputation is inaccurate — we aren't an interconnected global village at all. Most trade is extremely local, most people prefer it that way, and there might be a lot more money to be made in your neighborhood than anywhere else on earth.

So for those businesspeople who are worried sick about competing on a global scale, relax. As Dr. Helliwell relates, you might have more to worry about — and more to gain — in your own backyard. And for those who lambaste globalization as a curse and threat, simmer down. Your real power is local, and globalization may never be as bad as you think.

Gallup Management Journal: *Are our economies as globalized as we think they are?*

Dr. Helliwell: No. We tend to speak and write and think as though trade linkages, people linkages, and capital linkages are as solid globally as they are within countries. I had written and was thinking in that vein myself until fifteen years ago, when I came across a working paper by [Canadian politician and economist] John McCallum, who was making use of data from Statistics Canada after the Free Trade Agreement between Canada and the United States came about.

We already had data in Canada for trade movements among provinces, but the new numbers let McCallum compare the density, strength, and size of trade movements between provinces with those of trade movements between provinces and states. It's called a gravity model because, like the law of gravity, the attraction depends on the proportionality of the masses and the distance.

What McCallum discovered, greatly to his surprise, but even more to the surprise of other people in the economics profession and outside it too, was that trade intensities between Canadian provinces were twenty times as great as those between Canadian provinces and U.S. states.

GMJ: You don't mean somebody going from Toronto to Detroit to buy a Coke and coming back.

Dr. Helliwell: No, this is the actual shipments of goods. This is all the stuff that goes back and forth by trailers and trucks and airplanes. It does include the cross-border shopping, if you like, but that's peanuts compared to trade as we know it, which is wheat being grown in Nebraska and sold wherever it's sold.

The commonly held idea was that goods moved as intensely across national boundaries as they did within a country, yet here was very strong evidence that that wasn't true. The Canada-U.S. Free Trade Agreement of 1989 and its successor, NAFTA, have since affected McCallum's original finding, but local trade is still about ten times more intense. Among the countries of the European Union, which is essentially a single international market, trade is still five or six times greater within the EU countries than between them, in terms of these gravity model intensities.

GMJ: Did you have reservations about McCallum's research? It refutes a lot of what we believed, even ten years ago.

Dr. Helliwell: When I first saw it, I thought this is either the most important thing I've seen in international economics, or it's wrong. I spent half a dozen years trying to decide which. And in the end, I confirmed it, as did lots of other people in a number of ways, and it's starting to change the way people think about markets and international trade. There's a resulting literature building up, and it feeds back in one way or another into the wellbeing literature and the trust literature that says people carry on their commercial lives in a much more geographically constrained space than we thought they did.

GMJ: Why do people buy things close to home rather than farther away?

Dr. Helliwell: There are a few reasons. One is that people don't need as much variety as economists' models often assume they do. They only go far enough to get what they need. Another reason is that a lot of tastes are local; people actually like things of the sort that are nearby because they're used to them, and the local marketers are more able to spot what local people like and build products that are good for the local tastes, conditions, climate, and so on.

A third reason, which is somewhat more general, is that people have more confidence and faith in dealing with people they know and trust. Networks of personal contacts turn out to be extraordinarily important. Think about walking into a drugstore where the druggist is a friend, and you can simply ask him what you need. But when you go into a strange drugstore, you're by no means sure that they know anything, or are going to take your interests to heart, or won't put you on to the latest patent medicine. A friend will not sell you the Brooklyn Bridge.

GMJ: That sounds like a trust issue, as you've researched.

Dr. Helliwell: There are parallels we've discovered. Trust is important in the workplace, and the same kind of thing governs people's choices of where they trade and who they trade with. People are much more inclined to deal nearby than far away. Their networks are also more likely to be nearby than far away. Having discovered this and saying it was true for trade, we then researched whether it is true for all countries, and for services, for capital movements, and for migration.

GMJ: What did you find?

Dr. Helliwell: We found it was true more or less everywhere. All of the measures we had of intensity and connectedness are all much greater within countries than between countries, and they're all much greater within communities than among communities within a country. Regionalism lives on unheralded.

GMJ: There is an argument that globalization is better for everyone — that it's the precursor to democracy and raises living standards and material comfort to everyone it touches. Would you agree with that?

Dr. Helliwell: The kinds of things we're talking about are economic as well as social reasons for why people deal close at hand. What the data really say is that it's more costly to go farther away because you might get into risks that you don't know how to handle.

A lot of companies assume that there are pretty big economies of scale and that products made in one country are going to be big winners in some other country. They often find to their discomfort that it's not true — that by assuming that other people's tastes and systems are like yours, you can end up costing yourself a lot of money. That said, the opportunity to get access to world markets is very important, if what you're selling is really needed.

GMJ: So does local trade have benefits that globalization doesn't have?

Dr. Helliwell: Sure. Think of the environmental impact. It's a la mode to think in this way — to say "Tell me once again: Why is bottled water shipped across the world when nobody can tell the difference in the water itself?" But economically, a vibrant, quite diverse local community would probably be better insulated against shocks to its main source of livelihood.

GMJ: In that case, do you think government should promote local, interregional trade?

Dr. Helliwell: One of the nice things about most countries is that you don't need internal trade agreements. It is true we have an agreement on internal trade in Canada to break down some of the protectionist constraints that some provinces face, but basically that's pretty small potatoes. It would probably be a messy and not very workable government policy to try to subsidize local trade.

I think the important point is that economic activity is much more local than people thought it was. When some people first see those results, they think of all the gains to trade there would be if we increased international trade until its densities equal that of local trade. And my response is that's probably not the case. The current situation with high density of local versus national trade probably reflects an economic and social equilibrium that's a natural state, and there are good economic reasons for it. It doesn't mean we're passing on major gains from trade, and it doesn't mean we're losing out.

GMJ: Give me an example.

Dr. Helliwell: One way of demonstrating it is this: Suppose it were true that there were a lot of economic gains from getting global trade densities up as high as the intracountry ones are. If that were true, big countries would be much richer than small countries, because small countries are sort of bottled up inside themselves while big countries have much a bigger trading area within their borders.

But if you look across countries, that's not true. The simple correlation between country size and GDP per capita among the OECD [Organisation for Economic Co-Operation and Development] industrial countries is essentially zero, whether or not you include the United States, which is both the biggest and the richest. But it isn't true that the larger economies are richer than the smaller ones.

So that must mean that the gains from additional trade density among the industrial countries, even in terms of income per capita left on the table, are now not very great. That's another way of saying there's probably enough international trade going on already among the industrial countries. Some of the developing countries have clearly made some potential gains from trade, and people argue about what the right pace of that is. If somebody comes in and rips the resources out of the ground and leaves nothing much but corruption behind, then you'd say, "Wait a minute — that can't be the best way to develop that country."

GMJ: Do the benefits of high-density globalization outweigh the benefits of high-density local trade?

Dr. Helliwell: I think that it will always be the case — and should always be the case — that the local densities are higher than the international ones. But would we be better off if international trade densities grew much more relative to the local ones? There's a sense that these research results raise serious questions to the conclusions of both the globalists and the global protestors. Both of them agree that globalization is the norm, but they disagree on whether it's good or bad. This research says that globalization isn't anything as big as either camp thinks it is. And it certainly hasn't got the potential for good that the globalists think it has, and it doesn't remove the scope for local action in the way the protestors believe.

So you want to tell those who are against world trade to put down your placards, get back to your communities, and make them work, because you have lots of capacity locally to create tax rates that differ from other people's, public services that differ from other people's, social organizations that differ from other people's. Go and set them up, and get things right for the people whose lives interest you most.

THE OTHER $700 BILLION QUESTION

by Jennifer Robison

November 13, 2008

Say "$700 billion" to U.S. taxpayers, and they'll know exactly what you're talking about. That's the price tag of the rescue package passed by Congress to shore up the ailing U.S. financial system. And with a population of 300 million, that price tag amounts to about $2,300 for every man, woman, and child in the United States.

But there's another $700 billion problem facing the U.S. government, though it's not garnering the same public awareness as the financial bailout. It's hidden in the U.S. healthcare system, and it presents either a problem — or an opportunity — for taxpayers.

Where's the problem?

It's no secret that healthcare costs are on the rise in the United States — or that they take a substantial chunk out of the government's coffers every year. The Congressional Budget Office (CBO) reports that "Over the past 30 years, total national spending on healthcare has more than doubled as a share of GDP. . . . [A]ccording to CBO projections, that share will double again by 2035, to 31% of GDP. Thereafter, healthcare costs will continue to account for a steadily growing share of GDP, reaching 41% by 2060 and 49% by the end of the 75-year projection period." A good chunk of that spending will be on Medicare and Medicaid, which currently "accounts for about 4% of GDP, or 26% of total spending on healthcare. By 2035, those figures grow to 9% of GDP, or 30% of total spending on healthcare, and by 2082, to 19% of GDP, or 38% of total spending."

What's less readily apparent is that a significant portion of healthcare spending doesn't necessarily improve health. "A tremendous amount of what we pay is spent on things that don't actually do any good," says Princeton University's Angus Deaton, one of the world's foremost economists and a leader in healthcare economics. Peter Orszag, director of the CBO, agrees: If healthcare spending is currently at 16% of GDP, his analysis suggests that almost 5% of GDP — or about $700 billion annually — goes to healthcare spending that can't be shown to improve health outcomes.

And $700 billion might just be a portion of the problem. A recent report from PricewaterhouseCoopers estimated the wasteful spending in the entire healthcare system — not just the portion funded by taxpayers — to be up to $1.2 trillion of the $2.2 trillion annually spent on healthcare in the United States. This wasteful spending can be categorized into three waste "baskets": behavioral, clinical, and operational.

But where is that money going? That depends on whom you ask. Worry about rising healthcare costs is nothing new; government and business, not to mention taxpayers, have been fretting about the issue for decades. Meanwhile, solutions have come and gone without making any noticeable dent in the healthcare bill. But lately, the CBO has been taking a different tack at examining the $700 billion problem: It's using the principles of behavioral economics.

Behavioral economics

"We're aggressively monitoring developments in behavioral economics, both for our work in putting forward options to policymakers and in terms of evaluating the impact of proposals that are actually moving through the Congress," says Orszag. "Spending ten percent of GDP on healthcare services that don't improve health outcomes is nuts."

The CBO became so intently and rapidly interested in behavioral economics — which blends insights from psychology with more traditional, neoclassical economics — because it has the potential to reduce healthcare costs in ways that neoclassical economics simply can't. As most Economics 101 students could tell you, the underlying premise of neoclassical economics is that when most people are asked to make financial choices, they weigh the options rationally; emotions aren't a factor in their decisions.

Economists call getting your money's worth, whether in dollar value or in general happiness from the purchase, *utility*.

Where neoclassical economics falls short is in explaining irrational financial decisions that appear to have little or no utility, at least in neoclassical economic terms. Take cosmetic surgery, for instance. A nose is a nose is a nose, but many people have happily spent between $3,000 and $8,000 for cosmetic rhinoplasty though the original nose smelled as sweet. Neoclassical economics would say the utility from the nose job comes from the feeling of being more attractive.

The CBO believes that behavioral economics can not only help explain those unnecessary costs but point toward ways of reducing or eliminating them. Unlike neoclassical economics, behavioral economics assumes that human emotions play a role in influencing a consumer's spending decisions on anything from toothpaste to automobiles to rhinoplasty. And though the government doesn't care in particular how much utility a consumer gets from a prettier nose, it cares very much about the ever-increasing cost of tax-funded healthcare in general.

What this economic approach also can't explain entirely is the $3,000 to $8,000 price range for the cost of the surgery. In a neoclassical economic model, all hospitals would use the least expensive and most efficacious methods to create nicer looking noses. But clearly, though healthcare facilities have a financial incentive to keep costs down, some do, while others don't.

Of course, one of the costs involved is the surgeon's fee. Though plastic surgeons make more money in Manhattan than they do in Missoula, that explains only a portion of the price difference. "No one can find any explanation for why costs are so different across hospitals or regions of the country," says Deaton.

"The single most important determinant of our fiscal future is the rate at which healthcare cost per beneficiary will grow in the future," says Orszag. He notes that he "can't think of anything that's more important for the federal budget" than getting healthcare costs in line. And behavioral economics might be the answer to the $700 billion problem.

Overemphasizing personal experience

For example, the CBO's behavioral economic team is operating under the assumption that, as Orszag says, "Doctors are human beings. They're influenced by psychology, as is everyone." Emotion naturally affects the decisions that physicians and healthcare consumers make, and behavioral economics can help explain the degree to which emotions influence their decision making. The CBO's research indicates that a few behavioral economic findings, such as the importance of salience and social norms on decision making, may have the greatest impact on cutting waste.

That brings us to the topic of salience. We all recall things that are salient — thoughts or ideas that are memorable because they're prominent or recent — because they're top of mind. That applies to healthcare professionals as much as anybody else. "Doctors may overemphasize personal experience, especially recent events, in providing diagnoses and prescribing care because it is memorable and easily retrieved," says Orszag.

Studies indicate that this is accurate. In a recent presentation to the National Academy of Health Insurance, Orszag mentioned the results of a computer-based study that asked experienced vascular surgeons to monitor an expanding balloon, which simulated an asymptomatic abdominal aortic aneurysm. Some of the physicians were randomly assigned a bad outcome, while others were assigned a good one. The doctors then were given the same statistical information about future risk.

How did their experience affect the decisions these doctors later made? In Orszag's words, "Those who had experienced the bad outcome tended to choose to operate more quickly than those who had experienced the good outcome. Other evidence suggests that many doctors' imperfect knowledge of biostatistics makes it difficult for them to interpret clinical research, and that when they are presented with a positive screening test, they tend to overestimate the probability that a patient actually has a disease."

Overreliance on salience can be both expensive and dangerous because it short-circuits critical thinking. The CBO doesn't recommend that physicians stop relying on salience, however, because it's an ingrained human tendency. Instead, Orszag and his team believe that evidence-based practices could help overcome the effects of salience.

Replacing diagnoses and practices derived from short-term memory and experience with statistically verified or evidence-based standards solves two problems: Doctors have a standard to follow when evaluating each patient, and that would help eliminate variations in diagnostic and treatment practices.

Maggie Ozan-Rafferty, a healthcare expert, suspects that evidence-based standards would also help the medicine go down with doctors. "The more evidence-based the standards are, the easier it is for doctors to embrace them," she says. "It's a lot like airline standardization in the 1970s — seasoned pilots resisted it, but it improved operational efficiency and safety for everyone." These are the same goals shared by the healthcare industry today.

Normalizing norms

The CBO, however, believes that evidence-based recommendations should not come from economists or the government or even hospitals, because that's a sure way to create backlash among physicians and healthcare consumers. That's why the CBO believes that evidence-based mandates should come from medical associations. Deaton concurs. "Reorganizing a system from the way that people have always done it will meet resistance, for sure," he says.

Many times, however, healthcare workers dismiss such measures as "cookbook medicine," believing that their experience, knowledge, and skill are better guides to diagnosing individual cases than a checklist of medical processes. If that were true, however, there would currently be much less variance in treatment and in costs.

Nor are evidence-based standards the same thing as "HMO committee medicine," which healthcare providers as well as patients view with suspicion. Instead, it's the careful replacement of assumptions with well-researched standards that could eliminate unnecessary procedures and their attendant costs. "We do very little testing of what works and what doesn't in healthcare," says Orszag. "A shockingly large share of the healthcare services delivered is not backed by specific evidence that they work any better than anything else."

In Orszag's presentation to the National Academy of Social Insurance, he noted, "In the mid-1980s, the American Society of Anesthesiologists promulgated standards of optimal practice (both in procedures and equipment) after analyzing the most common sources of errors. Providers had an incentive to follow the standards because deviations from them made the imposition of malpractice liability more likely. After the standards were adopted, mortality rates fell to about 5 per million encounters, as compared with averages of over 100 per million during earlier periods. This experience thus provides a case study showing that aggressively promulgated standards backed by some incentives can alter a long-standing and suboptimal status quo."

This too falls in the province of behavioral economics: social norming. Mandates created by professional associations, for example, set norm patterns — if an association urges doctors to use a particular method because it achieves the best results, the doctor who doesn't use it is thus aberrant.

"Providing physician-level data on usage patterns and performance does seem to have some effect," says Orszag. "It's more effective when you tie it in with financial incentives, but simply providing information to physicians about their practice patterns relative to their peers does seem to affect their behavior. People don't want to be out of the norm."

Who's really paying the bill?

When making recommendations for reducing healthcare spending, it's easy to blame everything on healthcare providers. After all, they're the ones sending the bills. But that's short-sighted. For every healthcare decision, there's a patient granting approval. And it might be easier to grant that approval if medical treatment costs feel like they're someone else's expense.

The CBO suspects that as long as patients perceive that most healthcare spending comes from employers, insurers, or government rather than out of their wallet, they won't question the amount of money that is spent on healthcare. "Most of us don't realize how much we're actually paying for healthcare, and therefore we perpetuate this relatively inefficient system," says Orszag. "[But] if you told me that if we wrung some inefficiency out of the health system, my take-home pay would be three thousand dollars a year higher, that might generate more action than esoteric arguments about the long-term fiscal path we're on — and the fact that [the system is] a train wreck waiting to happen."

Looking through a behavioral economics lens suggests that healthcare costs should be more salient to the people paying them. This would require patients — as well as doctors — to know what procedures have been proven to produce the best outcomes, rather than relying on the social norms of whatever hospital they're in.

Figuring out where and how healthcare spending is being wasted could cause healthcare professionals and patients to speak out against useless practices. The collective response might even spur some action. But the crucial player in effecting change could well be business.

Businesses are uniquely positioned to understand the economic realities underlying the healthcare system. Businesses have communication outlets in place that can encourage employees to adopt health-conscious — and cost-conscious — behaviors. Business has political muscle. And businesses could well be spending their healthcare dollars on care that doesn't make anyone healthier.

So, though the research on applying behavioral economics to healthcare is preliminary, it's pointing in a compelling direction. When the evidence-based results are in, it might be up to business to start demanding more accountability regarding healthcare dollars. After all, the P in GDP comes from business — and many of the dollars in healthcare spending do too.

MAKING GREEN WHILE GOING GREEN

An interview with Interface chairman Ray Anderson
by Jennifer Robison

October 22, 2009

After Interface, Inc., adopted the cause of sustainability, the billion-dollar carpet company became even more profitable by going green, says Ray Anderson, its founder and chairman. Here are just a few of Interface's successes: Between 1996 and 2008, Interface cut its net greenhouse gas emissions by 71% in absolute tons (the Kyoto Protocol, in contrast, called for 7% reductions by 2012, which many said was impossible).

Yet over the same time frame, Interface increased sales by 66% and doubled its earnings, expanding its profit margins and propelling innovation. Interface also reduced greenhouse gas intensity (relative to sales) by 82%, wastewater stream by 72%, landfill-bound scrap waste by 78%, total energy usage by 44%, smoke stacks by 33%, and effluent pipes by 71%.

These efforts and others landed Interface at the top of GlobeScan's Survey of Sustainability Experts — all while saving the company $405 million. And since 2003, Interface has sold 83 million square yards of carpet with *zero* net global warming effect.

In this interview, Anderson explains how other companies can do what Interface has done. For starters, he says, cut waste. Ask for help if you need it; Interface has a consultancy called InterfaceRAISE that can assist businesses with their sustainability initiatives. Ask your suppliers to get on board, because that will have an environmental ripple effect and prevent you from inadvertently "green washing."

Just don't depend on government to be much help. As Anderson says, "All too often, a politician will jump to get in front of a parade, but politicians never start them." And when critics say environmental policies hurt business and cost jobs, don't believe that either: Interface has proven that what is lost of either can be replaced and then some. But, says Anderson in the following discussion, the only ones equipped to fix the ill effects of industry are the ones who cause them.

And they must. As Anderson says, the best way to avert climate-change disaster is to change the way we do business. Leading a company to achieve a zero environmental footprint is not only entirely possible, it's also highly profitable. And the moral and business arguments for doing so are impossible to deny.

Gallup Management Journal: Early in our conversation, you said that that the industrial system was ruining the biosphere and, left unchecked, would destroy it. But you also said that the only institution that could prevent this destruction was the same one doing the damage — the institution of business and industry.

Ray Anderson: Yes.

GMJ: Why not government?

Anderson: Governments don't lead, they follow. And governments move, well, ponderously at best. Business is doing the damage, and business can turn on a dime. Now, government has a role, and I hope the book [Anderson's book *Confessions of a Radical Industrialist*] makes that clear. So does the church, and so does education.

But business is far and away the most powerful player. And if business does not get on board, then it's basically over for homo sapiens because the industrial system as it is operating today is destroying the biosphere — and the biosphere undergirds civilization itself.

GMJ: Do you think business can change? And will it do so in time?

Anderson: It's a matter of survival and self-preservation. But it could already be too late. It really could. If it doesn't happen quickly enough, we can reach the point of no return, and that's especially true of global warming.

We're perilously close already to the point of no return, which is when the positive feedback loops begin to kick in and the methane released from the permafrost and the bottom of the ocean increase. The polar ice caps melt and no longer reflect heat; instead, this increases heat absorption, which in turn increases melting.

As for planting trees to absorb carbon dioxide, there's no way you can make up that difference by planting more trees; there's not enough land. So you've got a lot of bad things going on — and getting worse.

GMJ: Do you think that there's anything at all that government can do to help?

Anderson: Oh, yes. Government has its role. I think its greatest power is taxation. With an enlightened taxation policy, the government could change the world for the better. That step would force organizations to internalize their external costs by making them pay for their output, which is now paid for by everyone else. Then it becomes a cost of doing business. That's what cap and trade essentially does by setting a price on carbon emissions. The sooner we do that the better — and the higher the price of carbon the better.

GMJ: Won't that hurt business and cost jobs?

Anderson: I don't think so. I think it's going to create new industries, though it's probably going to drive some old ones out or change them. Petroleum and a lot of other industries certainly need to change what they're doing, but there are whole new fortunes to be made with new technologies once the playing field is level and we're all internalizing our external costs.

Wind power will be very competitive. Coal will disappear once the table is leveled. Nuclear doesn't stand a chance once the table is level. You take away the government subsidy right now on the insurance side of the nuclear industry, and the nuclear industry cannot get funded. Level the playing field, get the prices right, internalize the externalities, and you'd have a whole new game.

But only the government can do that. With its purchasing power, the government can move markets. With its taxation policy, the government can start whole new industries and quit propping up dangerous old ones.

The government is the biggest landlord in America, so it can change the whole scene on building construction. The government's regulatory regime has helped a lot, and thank goodness for it. We'd be in a hell of a shape if it weren't for regulations that have been put in place since Rachel Carson's 1962 book *Silent Spring*.

And the government ought to be raising the bar every day on its purchasing policy. It should be specifying climate-neutral products *today* because it's possible. And that would reward the early movers, and it would inspire innovation among the late movers — or the fast followers.

GMJ: You said that reading Paul Hawken's book The Ecology of Commerce *was an epiphany. How did you sell your epiphany to your board and to Wall Street?*

Anderson: Well, in the early years, we focused primarily on QUEST — the Quality Utilizing Employee Suggestions and Teamwork program that looked for and utilized in-house environmentally conscious ideas. We talked about the cost savings that we got from QUEST with our investors, at financial conferences, at analyst conferences, and with our board. Then we began to gain some traction on other areas of initiative such as renewable energy and recycling and so forth. And then we could show that our initiatives were highly profitable, and that's hard to argue with.

GMJ: Your sustainability initiatives required your suppliers to change their products and methods too. How did you get their buy-in?

Anderson: Thirteen or fourteen years ago, we said to our suppliers, "Here's where we're going. Those who come with us will get the business; those who don't, won't." And it changed our supply chain. There's a carrot and a stick here.

But we couldn't make any environmental claims as long as our suppliers didn't. That's "green washing." We really believe that green washing is the kiss of death. That transparent self-serving coat of green that a company spreads over what they're doing — the least sophisticated customer can see through that. And once they see through it, your name is mud. So honesty, integrity, authenticity, transparency — all of that comes wrapped up in one nice package.

GMJ: You said that companies that want to follow in your footsteps ought to start by cutting back on waste. Why?

Anderson: Because it's the way you get ahead of the cost curve — and there is so much low-hanging fruit. In the most efficient manufacturing or industrial company, you often will find allowances for off-quality, scrap, or waste. If you allow that, it will persist forever.

So we took the view that the only waste that's acceptable is zero. We define waste very broadly as any cost we incur that does not deliver a value to our customers — from off-quality to a misdirected shipment — that's waste. It's a bad debt that we don't collect. So when you define waste very broadly and go for zero, you start inventing new ways of eliminating waste. And if you think that's impossible, look around you: Nature's been doing it for three billion years.

GMJ: What's the next step?

Anderson: Then you sit down and figure out your own mountain — the mountain you have to climb to reach sustainability. Chances are, your mountain won't be all that different from my mountain, and you will find that innovation cuts across all faces. To fundamentally change the way you do business does require innovation, new thinking, new processes, and new products, so you've got to unleash that.

But study the mountain first of all. Figure out where you are and how far you have to go. Get the metrics. The numbers will show you what you need to know about where you're doing damage, where you can save money, where you can improve, and what you ought to do. And you might as well get started early. Very quickly, our people began to see the new way of thinking and get on board. And we are still doing it ourselves, with very little outside help. We've not been long on consultants.

GMJ: Right, but you have chemists and machinists on staff. What about companies with no scientists around?

Anderson: We offer a very useful service in InterfaceRAISE [a peer advisory service that offers guidance on driving business value through sustainability] in that unlike some consultants, we've actually done this ourselves. We're bringing that learning to the table, and we can shorten the learning curve for clients who want to climb their own mountain.

But there are a lot of consultants who can help you get your head straight, help you see the world differently, and that's good. Eventually, you have to take over your sustainability initiatives yourself because the other guy's no better than you and doesn't know more than you do.

I think in a business like ours, you would have to get to a certain size and scale before you could undertake what we've undertaken. In other industries where there's a whole lot less capital investment and a whole lot less material intensity built on fossil fuels, maybe it's possible to start [a sustainability initiative] when you start the business. A lot of food companies have done very well that way.

GMJ: You've made a business case for sustainability. Do you want to make a moral case too?

Anderson: Yes. I think they're closely related, and the moral case needs to be made. Who are we to destroy this creation? Who are we to assume it's ours to do with as we please? It doesn't belong to us; we belong to it.

That's the fundamental mindset shift that has to happen. This Earth's not infinite in its ability to supply the stuff to feed our industrial system. It's not infinite in its ability to absorb our waste. It's finite. You can see it from space — all you see is all you get. And who are we to deny future generations the right to exist? Who are we to use it all up in our generation and leave them nothing? What kind of morality is that? That's the height of selfishness, isn't it?

THE FED'S $600 BILLION GAMBLE

An interview with Gallup Chief Economist Dennis Jacobe
by Jennifer Robison

November 18, 2010

Response to the Federal Reserve's recent round of quantitative easing, a $600 billion effort aimed at boosting demand for Treasury bills and driving down interest rates to spur growth, has been swift and impassioned. Thomas Hoenig, president of the Federal Reserve Bank of Kansas City, called it a "bargain with the devil." "Everybody wants the U.S. economy to recover, but it does no good at all to just throw dollars from a helicopter," said Brazilian Finance Minister Guido Mantega in the *Financial Times*. What's more, leaders at the most recent G20 meeting expressed anger that the U.S. is effectively stimulating its exports at the expense of its international competitors.

The stock market, however, responded positively: On November 4, one day after the Fed's announcement, the Dow closed up 1.96%, the Nasdaq jumped 1.76%, and the S&P 500 ended the day up 1.93%.

So who's right? Those who think that the Fed's move will lead to runaway inflation, possibly sink the U.S. economy, and undermine global markets? Or those who believe this might be the beginning of the end of bad times?

Probably the second group, says Gallup Chief Economist Dennis Jacobe, Ph.D. In fact, the characteristically un-exuberant Jacobe goes so far as to say this might be "the turning point" for the U.S. economy. He hastens to add, however, that there are significant risks to quantitative easing — including higher commodity prices, inflation, and a currency war. He believes the risks pale in comparison to the potential benefits, though, especially if the U.S. focuses unwaveringly on job creation. That will take some effort, will, and optimism from consumers and the business community, as Jacobe says in the following interview.

Gallup Management Journal: Depending on who you ask, QE2 — as it's being called because it's the second round of quantitative easing in the last couple of years — will either doom us or save us. What do you think?

Dr. Jacobe: There's a lot of economic analysis that shows that it's risky, that argues it won't be effective, that suggests the first round didn't have as much impact as we may have wanted or anticipated, and that we'll get even less in the way of benefit now. When the Fed first announced it and I thought about it and talked about it, I was skeptical. But now, as I've seen its impact on expectations and behaviors, I think this really does have a chance to work.

GMJ: Why?

Dr. Jacobe: It's a psychological thing more than anything else. People on Wall Street have decided that you can't fight the Fed. If the Fed's going to keep pumping money into the system, if the Fed is going to drive up asset values, then that's what the Fed's going to do. That's why we saw a big increase in equities and the value of commodities such as oil, precious metals, and farm products since Federal Reserve Board Chairman Ben Bernanke spoke at an economic symposium in Jackson Hole, Wyoming in late August.

As a result, there's been some new optimism in the financial markets. That's because people are making money on Wall Street, U.S. exporters are seeing their competitive position improve, and international companies are seeing their earnings and profits go up. There's an increased demand for basic commodities that are a substantial part of the U.S. economy. That part of the export economy can see a good business environment going forward. The fact that the Fed has been so aggressive has convinced many businesses that things are going to get better for them. The stock market's boost has influenced them too — not to mention the mid-term elections.

GMJ: That's a lot of play from a single Fed decision that many people don't approve of.

Dr. Jacobe: That's correct. And many people don't agree with me that the Fed's determination to increase asset values is really driving economic improvement.

You know, recently, I went to the doctor for a problem I was having with one of my eyes. The doctor gave me some experimental medicine and told me to come back in a couple of weeks. When I returned, my eye had improved. When I noted that it appeared that the medicine had worked, he responded with a "maybe." He said that my eye might just have recovered on its own given a few weeks to heal.

That's the problem with assessing the Fed's actions, particularly when you are arguing that the policy has had a major impact based on expectations and behaviors. In turn, so the argument goes, improving expectations lead to an improved economy.

GMJ: So why do you think the Fed's "experimental medicine" is working while others don't?

Dr. Jacobe: Because Gallup's U.S. economic data, which are based on daily polling, allow us to see shifts in consumer perceptions and behaviors before they register in other, less immediate metrics. During late September and early October, Gallup's unemployment measure surged past double digits. Our consumer spending numbers showed a decline in spending, particularly among lower and middle-income Americans. Even our small-business polling showed that small-business owners were more pessimistic in July than at any time since August 2003.

In early October, Gallup's daily polling data suggested that the U.S. economy might be "hitting a wall" as it did in June 2010. It looked like consumers and businesses were becoming increasingly uncertain about the economy — like they weren't willing to make decisions — and the odds of a double-dip recession were increasing.

All that seemed to change in late October. We saw a surge in hiring that sent Gallup's unemployment numbers plunging. We also saw a sharp improvement in consumer optimism. I attribute much of this abrupt turnaround in consumer perceptions and business behaviors to the Fed's openness during September and October about its intention to drive up asset values. Wall Street surged, and the dollar's value plummeted. Global companies in the U.S. became more competitive. Even some of the economists who complained about the Fed's efforts seemed to acknowledge they would increase U.S. economic growth in the near term, if only on the margin.

In sum, Gallup data showed a sharp deterioration in the economy and then a strong rebound that the September and October monthly economic reports missed. If you look at traditional monthly economic trend data, you might argue that the U.S. economy has just begun to recover on its own. Gallup's daily economic data suggest to me that a sharp reversal in expectations and optimism has taken place — and I attribute much of it to the Fed's announced intention followed by its explicit statement that it would pursue a QE2 strategy.

Of course, I also think the mid-term elections may have played a role in changing perceptions. It seemed clear the Republicans were going to take over the House in early October. As a result, many major corporations could see that Americans were moving toward a politically divided government, which companies might perceive as posing less legislative and regulatory risk. With a divided government, there's less chance that Congress will pass aggressive actions in any area.

Based on my reading of Gallup's attitudinal and behavioral economic data, I think the combination of the Fed's QE2 and the change in the political environment has turned the psychology of the economy around. It's the first time I've seen the economic outlook this positive for quite a while.

GMJ: But this means the government's printing more money.

Dr. Jacobe: Yes.

GMJ: And using it to buy its own bonds.

Dr. Jacobe: Yes. We call it "monetizing the debt."

GMJ: Other people call it "inflation bait."

Dr. Jacobe: Well, there are big risks associated with the Fed's experimental policy. In its essence, the rapid devaluation of the dollar means inflation will occur. Commodity prices have gone up, food prices will go up, oil prices have gone up, gas prices should go up. As food and energy prices go up, American consumers will suffer. In turn, consumers could pull back on spending — purchase only necessities — and that could offset some of the benefits of increasing employment that QE2 will probably bring.

Further, people don't think about what this does to older Americans, when the economy basically has negative real interest rates. Many earning assets, such as savings accounts, won't earn much interest, so older Americans who live on their investments either must take on risk or see their income go down. It's a hard time for them, and it's a hard time for banking institutions because they can't lend money at any kind of attractive interest rate.

Ultimately, what the Fed is trying to do is generate price increases and avoid deflation. Now to some degree, the increases in commodity prices have been absorbed by foreign exporters. But the way the dollar is valued by some Asian currencies means that some of those inflationary factors have not translated into higher prices for many goods imported into the U.S. economy, and this situation could easily change, leading to much higher prices over time.

GMJ: Are there other risks associated with QE2?

Dr. Jacobe: There's the real possibility of something that might be seen as a currency war or even a trade war. This could happen if other countries decide they don't like the way the U.S. is devaluing its currency and start to devalue their own currencies. Many countries are already angry, as illustrated by their leaders' reactions at the most recent G20 meeting. They say the U.S. is taking advantage of the global situation; the U.S. is increasing its global exports and pumping up the commodity part of its economy, stimulating its exports at the expense of its international competitors. And they have a point. The U.S. is becoming much more aggressive and competitive internationally.

GMJ: Aside from inflation, could increasing commodity prices create asset bubbles?

Dr. Jacobe: Absolutely they could; they may already be doing so. If QE2 works, asset values will go up and people will start spending money again. But inflation could go wild because there's so much money out there. If that happens, how will the Fed pull that money back out of the global economic system? It becomes an enormous problem. Our experience with inflation is that once it gets going, it is very, very hard to stop. If we have too much money out there, we could get very rapid inflation increases.

The other danger is that uncontrollable bubbles form in various commodities, and that becomes a real problem for consumers. Depending on how job growth is going and whether the economy is actually expanding, the biggest short-term danger is a big jump in prices. To control surging prices, the Fed then must start increasing interest rates and pull money out of the system to pop those bubbles. They might have ideas and plans about how to achieve this goal while minimizing the damage to the global economy, but we're in totally uncharted waters.

Nobody ever thought that the Fed would actually buy debt and pump money into the economy to push up asset values. It's a tremendous experiment. Fed Chairman Ben Bernanke studied the Great Depression, and you can think of this as his anti-Depression strategy. That's why the policymakers and economists are reacting so strongly, because nobody knows what will happen over time.

GMJ: So once again, why do you favor this experimental Fed policy?

Dr. Jacobe: I think people's assessment of the Fed's new policy tends to differ depending on the time frame being considered and how you assess the risks involved. If you take a longer view, you might easily conclude that QE2 is a bad idea because of its long-term risks, including inflation and asset bubbles. This is particularly the case if you see today's unemployment rates as something the U.S. economy can live with for several years to come.

In contrast, a short-term view might be that the enormous risks involved are worth it: Without the Fed's efforts, the economy could stagnate or possibly slow further. Unemployment is likely to remain in the double digits for another year or two. The odds of a double-dip recession go up.

If the Fed's grand experiment works, we get an economy that starts to advance and we get jobs created. We may also get an inflation problem, and we take on the risk that we can minimize the damage if that happens. The worst result would be that the Fed tries to pump up the economy and we get inflation but we don't get economic growth. If that happens, then we have stagflation, and that's the worst outcome.

GMJ: Stagflation is a term that brings back dreaded memories from the 1970s.

Dr. Jacobe: Stagflation is a real worry. Still, the real problem right now is unemployment. In the short term, we have to do whatever it takes to get the economy going. Until recently, I thought the odds of stagflation were fairly high. I think the risk of that has diminished because we're at an economic inflection point. I think Americans, both consumers and businesspeople, are essentially an optimistic people. We've become a lot less optimistic over the last couple of years because of the recession and the financial crisis. But when the Fed is pumping money into the system and there's optimism that asset values will increase, that jobs will be created, and in turn, there will be economic growth, then basic American optimism and entrepreneurship will take over.

I think there's a reasonable chance that the Fed's strategy will work. I feel this more strongly than I had expected to because I think it's already affecting expectations. Gallup's most recent confidence measures are improving, and the job situation seems to be getting a little better. We're still a ways off before we can confirm that it's working, but so far, all the indications are good. The expectations built on QE2 and the change in fiscal policy associated with two-party rule are very positive.

GMJ: What will the impact be on small and medium-sized business?

Dr. Jacobe: Well, I think it's still a tough economic climate for small businesses. But we are at a turning point. If U.S. optimism continues, and if some of the bad things that can happen internationally like a currency war don't happen, and if people give this Fed policy a chance, then I think the outlook for small business and for the economy in general improves significantly, probably as soon as in the second quarter of 2011. On the other hand, if we retreat into the political and economic morass we've been in for the last couple of years, arguing about all kinds of things and not focusing on job creation, then I'm not as optimistic.

I think the correct action right now is to take whatever momentum the QE2 and the political change have generated in terms of America's expectations and optimism and build on them to create jobs. Whatever has to be done to improve the job situation is what we should be focusing on right now.

GMJ: What about fixing Social Security and deficits? Those problems are top of mind for many people right now.

Dr. Jacobe: Those are real problems and they're very important, but we don't need another dose of pessimism right now. What we need is for people to do whatever it takes to create jobs. Then after the economy gains some real positive momentum, we can talk about these serious issues in an economy that's expanding and with more people getting hired. Then we'll be in a better position to deal with inflation, deficits, Social Security, Medicare, and Medicaid. If we try to focus on those long-term problems before we take care of jobs in the short term, we'll get stagflation.

GMJ: And you thought we were getting close to that?

Dr. Jacobe: I did. Not too long ago, the situation was getting bad again. As I noted earlier, unlike many of the federal government's economic measures, Gallup monitors economic data weekly, not just monthly. Gallup's economic measures for late September and early October showed the economy slowing dramatically. At that time, in my view, the probabilities of the U.S. sinking back into a double-dip recession increased significantly. I was very worried about the outlook for the economy.

GMJ: Then why are so many people against QE2? Just recently, we've seen a group of Republican economists join with some Republicans in Congress to argue against this new policy and suggest that the Fed should not go through with it. In fact, House Republican Conference Chairman Mike Pence has just introduced new legislation to limit the Fed's role to controlling inflation because of QE2.

Dr. Jacobe: As we've discussed, some people think the economy is healing on its own. Others think the risks associated with such an experimental policy are just too great. Some simply argue it won't work. Further, I don't think there has been enough discussion about what happens to American society if unemployment remains in the near double digits — and one in five or more Americans are underemployed — for years to come. And, we continue to see global economic challenges such as the Irish debt crisis and China's efforts to combat inflation.

Most importantly, I don't think they're seeing what we're seeing with the Gallup Daily: The Fed's experimental action is already having an effect. We see unemployment dropping and hiring picking up. I think we'll see real estate values improve because quantitative easing makes hard assets more valuable, which in turn helps commercial real estate and homeowners. We have some positive momentum, and if people in Washington will focus on dealing with out-of-control federal spending while joining businesspeople and consumers in focusing on job creation, we've got a chance to have a much better year in 2011. This is the first time I've been really optimistic about the economic outlook in quite a while. I think we're at an inflection point here, and we have our best chance in years to turn this thing around.

CRISIS MANAGEMENT

MANAGING DURING A CRISIS

by Mick Zangari and Benson Smith

September 24, 2001

The next few weeks and months may be the most challenging time in any manager's career. Returning to "normal" will be easier said than done, as all of us try to cope with the horrific events of September 11 in our own way. For some, just trying to think about business at a time of tragic loss will seem inappropriate, while others will need to immerse themselves in work.

Although Gallup has been studying managers and employees since the 1960s, it's difficult to find an event that compares to the terrorist attacks on September 11. Nevertheless, we have observed many companies navigating through their own crises. Companies that have done the best at managing difficult situations have used these strategies: They continually evaluated the circumstances they faced as a result of a rapidly changing landscape, and they engaged their employees by sticking to fundamentals of great management.

Evaluate your situation

One of the reasons returning to normal may be difficult is because we may not know what normal is. Everyday life has changed dramatically and will never be quite the same. Certain industries will see a potentially devastating impact. The airline and travel industries already appear to be in this group, and many other industries may feel a short-term impact as decision making slows. There will be a ripple effect throughout the economy as businesses with customers among the affected industries experience the impact of change.

Other industries will find themselves pushed to meet new customer demand. Governments and businesses are likely to spend more on security and surveillance, but other industries also will see an uptick in spending. If Americans are reluctant to take back to the air, or they postpone their travel plans, what will they spend those dollars on instead? What will be the ripple effects of any changes in spending habits?

At this point, no one knows the answers to any of these questions. Often the experts guess wrong, and circumstances turn out to be very different from what we anticipate. The best companies, when faced with a crisis, continue to examine the situations they face until they have a clear picture of what normal means. In the interim, keeping your employees engaged is critical.

Engaging employees during adversity

Setting clear expectations is important under any circumstances, but it's even more so in a crisis. People who deal with crowd evacuations, for example, find it necessary to repeat simple and obvious instructions over and over again. Phrases like "Keep moving" or "Don't stop" are essential elements of an evacuation process. Why is this so? Aren't these things obvious?

In times of confusion and uncertainty, people require crystal-clear expectations of what they need to do. No matter how carefully you set expectations for your employees before September 11, no doubt they have changed. Your annual budgets may no longer make sense. Your daily patterns may be interrupted, or your customers may need special help, reassurance, and assistance.

Redefining expectations in response to a crisis is absolutely essential. This takes work and thought, and sometimes we as managers dodge this responsibility with watered-down expectations. Don't tell employees, "Do the best you can." A crisis is no time for vagueness. Meaningful expectations, though, cannot be set without employee input.

Seek opinions

We know from our research that an employee's connection to an organization is linked to a sense that his or her opinions seem to count.

As you try to understand a rapidly changing landscape and set new expectations, listen carefully to feedback from your employees.

While one of our client companies was going though a crisis, Peter M., a senior executive, made this observation: "More than ever before, we needed the information our workforce provided us. They were visiting with our customers and suppliers every day. We relied on them to tell us what was going on and to help us develop the right strategies."

Kathy C. worked for a company that took a very different approach when its industry was in trouble. "We kept getting memos from the home office that told us, 'Everything is okay. It's business as usual.' I wondered, 'Who are they trying to kid?' Everything was far from okay, and I was reminded of that on every customer call I made."

As you reshape your company's plans, you need to include your workforce in the information-gathering process and ask for their suggestions on what the best recovery strategies might be.

Use mission to unite your workforce

Your company's mission also can sustain employee engagement. We all work for many reasons, and a paycheck is just one of them. During a time of crisis, those other reasons assume paramount importance. We rally around the countries, causes, and companies we believe in.

In difficult circumstances, we can show our employees that our company's mission statement is not merely empty words. Instead, it embodies values that are important, ones we can fall back on when times are tough.

On September 11, U.S. citizens experienced an attack on our economy and our way of life, much more so than on our military strength. An important and vital response to this attack is to rebuild our economy. A short-term military action won't accomplish this. The process of rebuilding the economy will happen company by company, job by job, and person by person.

Great managers can find a way to harness each person's overwhelming desire to help by showing them how their job contributes to the rebuilding process.

Show employees that you care

Harnessing that energy takes more than a sense of shared values. It takes a relationship. Our research clearly shows that people don't work for companies — they work for people. They work for their supervisor or their manager. They work for you.

All of us, in some way, have been touched by recent events. All us have a unique way to cope with our feelings and to put events in perspective. Great managers understand this, and they resist the temptation to rush their employees through this process. A manager who sends mixed messages — who tells his employees, "You are important to me," but whose actions say, "I am much too busy to bother with you right now" — will lose credibility with his employees.

A time of crisis is a time to build relationships. It can be a time to show what you and your company really stand for. And it can be a time to tap into values that are more important to us than the numbers on our paycheck.

Clarity, not complexity

If all this seems simple — it is. Difficult challenges do not usually require complicated solutions, but rather straightforward ones.

Our role as managers and leaders is to minimize confusion, not add to it. No situation is so bad that it cannot be made worse by overreaction. Take stock of your situation, but understand it may change dramatically in a few short weeks and months.

Set clear expectations. No battlefield commander says, "Do the best you can." Instead, he says, "Take that hill," or "Knock out that bunker." Be clear. Be specific.

Don't pretend things are normal if they are not. Give your employees good information about what's happening, and ask them what they're hearing from customers or suppliers. They are often your best source of information, and they need to express their observations and opinions.

Finally, use this opportunity to show what your company mission is all about. You will build relationships that will endure long after the crisis has passed.

THE ECONOMIC CRISIS: A LEADERSHIP CHALLENGE

by Jennifer Robison

May 12, 2009

"Those executives flying around in private jets and buying fourteen-hundred-dollar trash baskets are making every leader look bad," says a manager at an automotive company in the southern United States. "We've lost twenty-five percent of our workforce in my division, so I'm putting in an extra twenty hours a week or more. Yet my division head is on her second cup of coffee when I get in, and I have no idea what time she leaves at night."

In the toughest economy the world has faced since the Great Depression, most organizational leaders aren't taking time to ponder the upholstery of their antique desk chairs; most are trying to make it through the day. And the economy is likely to get worse before it gets better: Most economists say the U.S. GDP will turn around by mid-2009, but the unemployment rate will continue to climb through 2010.

That reality presents two discrete leadership challenges: keeping a company on track while the global economy is falling apart and keeping it functional until the economy recovers. Right now, most executives are focusing on the former. "Around the world, there's a giant ball of fear," says Tom Rath, Gallup global practice leader and coauthor of *Strengths Based Leadership*. "Almost all leaders are focusing on just keeping their companies together."

That's an essential short-term strategy. Senior executives must get their managers and employees through the first of the worst before they can implement long-range plans. But leaders must also cope with anxious Wall Street investors, legitimately nervous staff, an uncertain future, and consumers who are spending warily. Keeping a company together is quite a feat under such conditions — but employee engagement can help in this effort.

Engagement = profit

Employee engagement is an emotional attachment between an employee and his or her workplace. Employees are more likely to become engaged when 12 key psychological needs are met, such as feeling cared for, having necessary equipment, and knowing what's expected. Gallup measures employee engagement using an assessment called the Q^{12} that includes 12 items — one to represent each of those 12 needs. (See "The 12 Elements of Great Managing" in the Appendix.)

In a time when jobs are scarce and employees with jobs are unlikely to jump ship, why should companies care about whether their employees are engaged? Because research by Gallup and others shows that boosting engagement links to financial performance in several ways:

- Business units in the top quartile of employee engagement have 12% higher customer advocacy, 18% higher productivity, and 12% higher profitability than business units in the bottom quartile.

- Business units in the bottom quartile, in contrast, have 51% more inventory shrinkage, 31% to 51% more turnover, and 62% more accidents than business units in the top quartile.

An engaged workforce can also boost stock price, which is of great importance in a volatile market. Gallup research has shown that organizations with more than four engaged employees for every one actively disengaged employee saw 2.6 times more growth in earnings per share (EPS) than did organizations with a ratio of slightly less than one engaged worker for every one actively disengaged worker. And growth in EPS for organizations in the top quartile of employee engagement outpaces the EPS growth for companies in the bottom quartile by 15.6%.

"A bad economy is the test of an organization's culture," says Jim Harter, Ph.D., Gallup's chief scientist of workplace management and wellbeing and coauthor of *12: The Elements of Great Managing*. "In good times, consumer demand can disguise the lapses in productivity that disengagement causes.

But in bad times, there isn't any way to hide the performance problems of disengagement."

Reaching out

When a company is in trouble — as many are these days — employee engagement can be the difference between surviving or not. Keeping engagement alive in a good market takes effort and commitment from the top. Leaders must do even more to keep their managers and employees engaged when bad economic news can distract or frighten employees.

First, leaders must keep managers focused on meeting their employees' emotional needs with unflagging predictability, especially the first six elements of the Q^{12}. "Outside events affect workgroups," says Scot Caldwell, a Gallup learning solutions consultant. "The first six elements can be used to address, coach to, and respond to those events. They provide both a barometer of and a way to respond to change."

But leaders shouldn't stop there. Fear and uncertainty can erode an organization's wellbeing, but there are steps leaders can take to build confidence and avoid the paralysis or stagnation caused by relentless bad news. Helping their employees feel secure and cared for, providing clear communication, and leading with honesty and hope can go a long way toward bolstering engagement.

Security

Even if your company hasn't been forced into implementing layoffs or pay freezes, your employees know that other businesses have — and that may be affecting them. "The big challenge to executives right now," says Rath, "is that uncertainty breeds fear. And fear feeds on itself."

Leaders can't entirely quell those fears. They can't control the economy or predict the future, so they can't assure workers that everything is fine and always will be. But they can promote a feeling of stability from day to day, and that creates a sense of security *and* engagement. Employees who are highly confident about their company's financial future are nine times more likely to be engaged than those with lower confidence, according to Gallup research. So don't change what you don't have to, and maintain office traditions as much as possible, while keeping in mind that public displays of executive belt tightening can avert an "us versus them" mentality in the ranks.

A leader's biggest short-term problem can be the paralysis that comes from panic. Predictability is a good antidote for that. "Make sure your systems and processes continue to function consistently and that your approaches don't vary widely because of changed circumstances," says Barry Conchie, a Gallup leadership expert and coauthor of *Strengths Based Leadership.* "Try to exude as much of a 'business as usual' feel, and meet people's needs for stability and security so that while everything else is changing, there are some predictable elements in life and in work."

Caring

The lifeblood of employee engagement is caring — the feeling that your boss or someone at work cares about you personally, that someone encourages your development, and that the people around you care about the work they do. While caring is always an essential aspect of engagement, when workers feel threatened or insecure about their jobs, knowing that someone cares is enormously important — and individualization is implicit in caring.

"You can't show people you care if you don't know them, so you have to spend time with people one on one," says Harter. "Talk with your employees about their home and work situations. Don't make assumptions at a distance. Those things are always important, but they're even more so now."

Even in the best of times, many leaders are hesitant to show that they care about their employees. They may think that expressions or demonstrations of caring will undermine professionalism, make difficult decisions harder, or have a negative impact on employees' performance. In fact, that's wrong. Gallup research shows that the more leaders or managers know about their individual employees, the higher those workers' performance will be.

Yet when companies are laying people off, retreating from personal connections is a natural self-protective stance. How can you ask a worker about her kids today when you suspect you'll be pink-slipping her tomorrow? But cutting people off can make them more insecure — and make bad news harder to hear too.

"Caring doesn't mean that you run away from difficult decisions about cutting jobs or restructuring. Caring means the way that you communicate, how you involve others in tough discussions, the value that you show for people, and what you do to people when the worst happens," says Conchie. "I think the organizations that will lose significant numbers of their people, yet still retain that sense of compassion, are the ones that will recover engagement quickest."

Showing that you care for your workers can keep engagement alive. Remember, however, that some of the people who most need you to care are your managers. They're stretched very thin these days, they often must bear the brunt of downsizing decisions, and they're the ones taking care of frontline staff. "Leaders need to take care of their managers," says Denise McLain, Gallup principal. "The most important and best thing leaders can do is to let managers know they're valued and to tell them what they're doing right. Right now, they really need to hear that."

Integrity and honesty

"Respect the people you work with enough to give them up-to-the-minute information about how your business is doing," says Shane Lopez, Ph.D., Gallup senior scientist in residence and a leading researcher of hope. "I think this issue of 'We don't want to scare them' is paternalistic."

It's not only paternalistic, it's counterproductive. Employees *are* scared — and with good reason. They know that the economy is bad, that it's affecting their company, and that it might affect them. Sugarcoating the truth, or avoiding it entirely, stokes employee fear and only makes things worse.

Employees need to know how their organization is doing, and leaders are responsible for delivering that message, no matter how bad the news is. "There is almost always a need to convey the truth about the circumstances that you're in, and sometimes that news is pretty harsh," says Conchie. "If an organization's leaders can be honest and direct in the expression of harsh realities, then they'll also go a long way toward either retaining or improving levels of engagement."

Delivering news honestly shows that leaders respect their workers, and that promotes trust, which they will need in the days ahead. Lopez suggests that executives issue memos about the company's situation broadly and systematically so that the information is predictable and reaches everybody. In any case, it should be truthful — even if the truth is that leaders need to stop, take stock, and develop the next plan.

"There's a difference between not knowing exactly what to do and disengaging from the problem," says Conchie. "Most leaders worth their salt have got some pretty good ideas about what to do but don't know how all the variables will play out. It's okay to be honest by saying, 'These are things that we're thinking of doing. Here are the uncontrollable variables. Here's the rationale. And here's how I think it would help.' I think that's perfectly permissible. That is the way to operate with integrity."

Hope

In the United States, 5 million people have lost their jobs since the recession began. Some of the sturdiest, most profitable companies in the world are laying people off. The housing market is struggling, it's difficult to get a bank loan, and consumer confidence is languishing — between February 2008 and May 2009, 51% to 85% of consumers have classified current economic conditions as negative, according to daily Gallup Polls.

"We haven't even crested our wave of fear. And that's what companies need to manage today," says Lopez. "The challenge today is managing fear, then building hope about goals that we can all believe in." Instilling hope is an economic imperative for leaders. Gallup has found that 69% of employees who strongly agreed that their company's leadership made them "feel enthusiastic about the future" were engaged in their jobs, compared to just 1% of employees who disagreed or strongly disagreed.

Again, it's a mistake to condescend to employees or fudge the truth. But no matter how bad things are or will get, there certainly is reason for hope — eventually the economy *will* improve. Employees just need to know how their company plans to survive during the downturn. They need to know what to focus on to help set it up to succeed. They need to know that leaders are doing whatever they can to protect jobs. And they need to know what the market wants and how to meet it. Put simply, employees need a reason to hope.

"Prepare for the worst and for the best," says Rath. "There's a ton of research that indicates that followers need hope and stability more than anything. Without hope, it's hard to get by at all."

Shore up, then dig down

Much has been said, frequently in coarse language, about leaders like former Merrill Lynch CEO John Thain. While Merrill Lynch's stock was sliding and major layoffs were looming, Thain spent $1.2 million decorating his office. He didn't help his cause by making a late disclosure of billions in fourth-quarter trading losses and awarding billions in bonuses shortly before Bank of America took over his company.

But little has or will be said about leaders like the division head mentioned at the beginning of this article. She's working endless hours, making painful decisions in uncertain conditions, and putting her career on the line to keep her company afloat during these dark days. That's true of many leaders now, and they aren't making headlines.

Still, no matter how hard these leaders work, they can't control the economy. One thing they can influence, however, is employee engagement. Fortunately, that's also something that drives profitability and productivity — two factors vital to businesses right now. We may not hear about the leaders who are advancing engagement in their companies during these bad times, but we don't need to. We'll know who they are when the recession ends. They'll be the ones with healthy businesses.

What Leaders Should — and Shouldn't — Communicate

Communication in rough times is critical, and it must be truthful, open, and proactive. But that doesn't mean leaders shouldn't weigh their words carefully. According to Gallup experts, here are some suggestions for what leaders should communicate — and what they should keep under their hats.

Don't talk to workers like you would talk to analysts. Wall Street needs to know the details of your financials and your projections. They want hard numbers. Employees, however, need your humanity. Tell analysts that your layoffs represent a small fraction of your workforce. Tell employees that letting people go was the last thing you wanted to do.

Don't let the rumor mill take over. As bad as things are, the rumor mill will always make them sound worse. So communicate regularly through every available channel, and — whether the news is good or bad — make sure the message is consistent across all channels. Tell employees everything you can about your company's finances and how they affect individual employees.

Talk about the greater good. Your business strategy, tactics, and changes are meant to preserve the health of your company. Let employees know when hard decisions are necessary to ensure your company's survival, especially painful changes like job cuts.

Don't let employees hear bad news first on CNN. When a companywide decision has been made, employees need to hear it first and from you. In tough times, employees need a sense of security, and they won't get that if they are the last to know.

Be visible. Employees need to see you to believe you. They can't trust that you understand their troubles if you're not visible in their world. Make the rounds, listen to people, and ask about their situations. Workers will know you care, and you'll learn things you couldn't have learned otherwise.

Explain how the economy is affecting your company in words everyone can understand. Don't assume that your employees know esoteric financial terminology — but don't talk down to them either. It's wise to explain why, for instance, a lower share price doesn't necessarily mean downsizing or how a leveraged buyout will affect personnel.

ENGAGEMENT, WELLBEING, AND THE DOWNTURN

by Jennifer Robison

August 5, 2010

As many as 14.6 million Americans are unemployed, according to the U.S. Department of Labor. That means 14.6 million people have been dealing with the losses that come with unemployment: the loss of financial stability, of identity, and of their normal daily routine.

Emily Wright dealt with these losses for a whole year. She lost her management job in consumer marketing in September 2008 and didn't find another one for exactly a year. "It was scary," Wright says. "Some of the others who were laid off didn't know how they were going to be paying the mortgage that month." Fortunately, Wright had six months' worth of living expenses saved, and she received unemployment benefits. But her income and savings barely covered her scaled-down cost of living.

"I joked, kind of, that I was a drain on society because I was taking government money," says Wright. "I *never* thought it would take this long to get a job. I finally reached a point of wondering how many months I could get by if I sold my car, if I sold my house. By August 2009, I knew that if I didn't get hired soon, I'd be taking a job at the mall."

Effects of stress

Wright's experience is typical for the recently unemployed. But stress about work is not an unusual reaction for people *with* jobs either. In 2007, the American Psychological Association reported that 74% of Americans said that work is their main source of stress, up from 59% the year before.

There are many ways managers and executives can help employees manage their stress: frequent, honest, and informative communication; involving the workforce in understanding new strategies and explaining how they're essential to the new plans; an emphasis on recognition for good work; and a focus on hope. "Everything we've seen suggests that trust, compassion, stability, and hope are what people need from leaders in times of trouble," says Jim Harter, Ph.D., Gallup's chief scientist of workplace management and wellbeing and coauthor of *12: The Elements of Great Managing.*

A Gallup study found that while those tactics work, they're most effective with an engaged workforce. Workplace engagement is the core of the unwritten social contract between employers and employees. It begins at a local level, usually in the relationship between a manager and his or her employees. Engagement results from the fulfillment of 12 universal human needs. And when those needs are met, workers are engaged. (See "The Three Types of Employees" and "The 12 Elements of Great Managing" in the Appendix.)

A recent Gallup study examined the attitudes of U.S. workers as the country moved through the recession. Gallup asked respondents about their wellbeing, whether they had experienced changes in their job status, and whether their company had experienced downsizing or layoffs. Respondents were also asked Gallup's 12-item employee engagement assessment, the Q^{12}, which determines an individual's level of engagement with his or her workplace.

Engagement remained relatively stable as the recession picked up steam. In July 2008, Gallup found that 31% of employees were engaged, 51% were not engaged, and 17% were actively disengaged. Those numbers changed only slightly in March 2009: 30% were engaged, 52% were not engaged, and 18% were actively disengaged. Although overall engagement levels dropped only slightly, Gallup's research revealed lower scores on specific elements of engagement.

For instance, scores on the recognition and praise item increased from July 2008 to March 2009. This change could be because "managers are leveraging the non-monetary means they have to motivate their workforces during a down economy," Harter says. "Recognition keeps morale up," says Denise McLain, a Gallup senior consultant. "Companies are asking more and more of their employees. They're taking away staff, they're taking away inventory, they're even taking away hours. So when you think about asking people to do so much more with so much less, they need something in return. And recognition is one of the things that can help with that."

At the same time, scores on several other Q^{12} items dropped significantly. Employees may have issues with clarity of expectations, for example. "As the economy changes, layoffs happen, and people change their roles," Harter says, which could explain the lower scores on the "knowing what's expected" item. "There is a lack of certainty about the future, and managers may have to continually clarify expectations to counter that during these times."

The research also revealed lower scores on four other Q^{12} items: talking about progress, opportunities to learn and grow, a connection with the mission of the company, and the opportunity to do what I do best. Managers might want to put more emphasis on these items to help employees stay engaged and productive, Harter suggests.

Effects on employee wellbeing

Gallup also asked employed Americans about their job status and wellbeing. Based on their responses to questions about their life, their wellbeing was classified as "thriving" (strong, consistent, and progressing), "struggling" (moderate or inconsistent), or "suffering" (at high risk).

The study found that changes in job status can affect people's perceptions of their wellbeing. The vast majority of workers (93%) were employed full time in July 2008 and were still employed full time in March 2009. Among these workers, the percentage with thriving wellbeing dropped two percentage points (from 53% to 51%) over this time frame. Among the 4% of workers who experienced a change in job status from full time to part time from July 2008 to March 2009, the percentage with thriving wellbeing dropped three percentage points (from 46% to 43%). But the percentage with thriving wellbeing dropped dramatically among the 3% of workers who went from being employed full time to being unemployed: from 37% to 29%, or eight percentage points.

Workers' perception of their wellbeing also differed depending on their engagement level. In terms of their wellbeing, among engaged workers, 60% were thriving, 37% were struggling, and only 3% were suffering. Among workers who were not engaged, 47% were thriving and 48% were struggling, while 5% were suffering. Actively disengaged workers, on the other hand, showed much higher percentages of suffering and struggling wellbeing levels: only 28% were thriving, while 60% were struggling and 12% were suffering.

Long road back

The more engaged workers are, the more productive they are and the more secure they are. It's a cycle that Emily Wright, the consumer marketing manager, is experiencing right now. After being out of work for a year, she got a similar marketing job. That job, however, requires a 200-mile daily commute and offers a 40% pay cut for work she mastered a decade ago. "But they need me here. And I'm going to take this company to a whole other level."

EXACERBATING THE FEAR OF LAYOFFS

by Steve Crabtree

October 28, 2010

Employees' fears of layoffs and downsizing, which can induce anxiety even in the best of times, have been aggravated by the stormy economic climate of the past two and a half years. Those fears can be exacerbated when employees work in an environment characterized by low trust, poor communication, or lack of clarity about expectations.

When layoffs or downsizing occur, engagement levels may drop as employees mourn the loss of friends and wonder if they might be next. To test that assumption, Gallup interviewed more than 6,900 adults who were employed full time or part time in July 2008, then interviewed the same respondents again in March 2009 as part of its research into the State of the American Workforce: 2008-2010. Overall, employee engagement levels among this group changed little between the two surveys. In July 2008, 31% were engaged and 17% were actively disengaged. Eight months later, the numbers were similar: 30% were engaged and 18% were actively disengaged.

In the March 2009 interview, Gallup asked respondents whether their organization had experienced layoffs or had downsized. About half (46%) said their organizations had gone through layoffs or downsizing since they were interviewed eight months earlier. The analysis compared changes in engagement scores among these employees with changes among the remaining respondents — those whose organizations had not experienced layoffs or downsizing.

In both 2008 and 2009, respondents who worked in organizations that experienced layoffs or downsizing were less likely to be engaged in their jobs than those who worked in organizations where no layoffs or downsizing occurred. That would seem obvious; it's likely that the work environments in downsizing companies were more stressful. But this finding may also reflect that organizations with more engaged employees tend to perform better financially than their competitors, so they were less likely to lay people off in the eight months between surveys.

However, the purpose of the analysis was to compare the *changes* in engagement levels among workers whose organizations had been through layoffs and those whose organizations had not. Here there was less difference: The ratio of engaged to actively disengaged workers worsened marginally between 2008 and 2009 among workers whose organizations had laid people off as well as among those whose organizations had not.

How Did Layoffs and Downsizing Affect Remaining Workers?

In July 2008, Gallup interviewed more than 6,900 adults employed full time or part time, then interviewed the same respondents again in March 2009. Gallup analyzed the changes in engagement levels among workers whose organizations had been through layoffs and those whose organizations had not. For both groups, the ratio of engaged to actively disengaged employees worsened only slightly from the first to the second measurement. This ratio was higher in both 2008 and 2009 for employees whose organizations had not been through a layoff or downsizing.

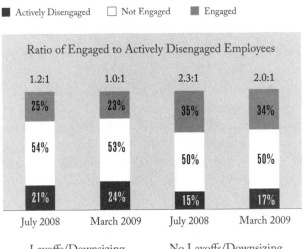

Though the overall engagement results were relatively stable among both groups, there were significant differences regarding a few individual engagement items. These differences offer insights into specific effects of layoffs and downsizing:

- *In organizations that experienced layoffs or downsizing, employees reported a significantly greater decline in the perception that they have the materials and equipment they need to do their jobs and that they have the opportunity to do what they do best every day.* In downsized workplaces, employees may be asked to increase their productivity and take on additional — and perhaps unwelcome — tasks and responsibilities. For example, in a department with fewer workers, the "survivors" may be getting stuck with a greater workload.

- *Scores on a third item also declined significantly among workers in organizations that had been through layoffs: "The mission or purpose of my organization makes me feel my job is important."* This may reflect disillusionment among employees who have seen their coworkers let go.

What can managers do?

In workplaces where layoffs or downsizing has occurred, managers shouldn't allow turmoil in the external economic environment to distract them from their employees' needs. Focusing on these workplace dynamics may help put employees' minds at ease in the wake of downsizing:

- **Manage human resource challenges with employees' talents clearly in mind.** After a round of layoffs, managers may transfer work and responsibilities to their remaining employees without considering whether that additional work plays to those employees' talents and strengths. Doing so may compound the anxiety that the layoffs generate. Worse, employees may get "locked in" to roles that they aren't particularly suited for, reducing their long-term engagement and the overall efficiency of their workplaces.

- **Communicate the organization's mission and strategy clearly and often.** Reassuring workers about the organization's commitment to its long-term goals and principles can help them focus on stability rather than the changes taking place around them.

The stress that accompanies layoffs can cause managers to adopt a command-and-control mentality — a mindset that sets aside the needs and opinions of employees to focus on short-term productivity. This tendency may be particularly strong among middle managers, who may be asked to accomplish more with fewer people and who may simultaneously be worried about keeping their own jobs.

It's important to avoid such a reaction for two reasons. First, by heightening stress and negativity among team members, managers in "survival mode" may risk lowering rather than increasing productivity. Second, input from all employees is particularly important in lean times as organizations seek creative solutions to the challenges they face.

LEADING CHANGE

GOOD TO GREAT? OR LOUSY TO GOOD?

by Jim Clifton, Chairman and CEO of Gallup

June 9, 2005

My phone rings, and it's the division president of a large telephone company. She offers to replace our current Gallup long-distance lines for a quick 10% savings. This means a lot of money to us. And the telephone lines we need in the United States and around the world are a commodity. They all seem to work well and sound fine, regardless of the long-distance carrier we use. As we are a business with serious employee owners, it seems an easy decision to dump our longtime partner for one offering a significantly lower price.

I call our top managers in the IT department, Phil and Phil, and they say they will study it. They soon get back to me with their recommendation to stay with our current technology partner — Partner A. Phil and Phil are super-competent technology leaders at our company, and I was sure that they would have a great explanation.

Phil and Phil described in detail the innovations that Partner A has brought to the table over the past few years, including a deal-saving technology breakthrough that helped us rescue one of our best accounts, a large and demanding retailer. They felt that Partner A brought more to the table than just global lines. This partner helped us win, save, and grow accounts.

Phil and Phil reported that Partner A knew our industry as well as or better than our own people. They also informed me that Partner A was re-engineering our global teleconferencing to VOIP and building a new state-of-the-art interviewing system throughout the 25 European Union states that would quickly make us the technology leader in our field in the

EU. And they are in the middle of helping us compete to win a complex project in Brussels.

Higher margin business from current customers

If you've ever wondered what, exactly, is meant by the financial term "organic growth," there is no better example than this story. Organic growth occurs when an organization like Partner A creates more transactions with its current customer base and with continuously growing margins. Organic growth first occurs by retaining current customers, then by increasing transactions with them. Whether your company has 100 customers or several million, organic growth occurs when you increase the amount of sales with your current customer base.

Many executives think that an organic growth strategy is the opposite of an acquisition strategy. They are not opposite as much as they are extremely different, and they require extremely different approaches and cultures to execute them successfully.

Let's go back to the story about Partner A for a moment. Partner A has developed a "fully engaged" relationship with our company. Fully engaged customer relationships like these embody four distinguishing characteristics:

1. Fully engaged customers *renew*. You keep them.

2. Fully engaged customers *buy more often*. You have more transactions per customer per year.

3. Fully engaged customers *create positive conversations* in your organization and in the market. They create leads.

4. Most importantly, fully engaged customers will *pay a higher margin*. Put a better way, they value their total partnership with your organization rather than just its price.

Partner A perfectly executed an organic growth strategy. An organic growth strategy succeeds when companies maximize relationships with current customers. This is very different — and much more powerful — than losing existing customers based on price, then replacing them with new customers based on price.

What Wall Street is missing

Financial analysts often miss this crucial point: Lousy companies can churn through customers and still show sales growth through replacement. But accounting reports won't reveal their huge customer turnover. This cycle — losing customers based on price, then getting new customers based on price — is what I call "riding the razorblade," and it has been the unspoken strategy of most companies over the past 20 years.

Company leaders talk a good game about growth at state-of-the-company speeches. But then they go right back to their offices and continue okaying new contract lows to hold customers or win replacement business. They do this largely because Wall Street has not really caught onto the deep implications of organic growth and how to spot it, even though it remains the best single metric to predict sustainable growth, sustainable profit, and share growth. If someone said to me, "In your 30 years of studying customer data, what is the indicator or single metric that is the key to buying or selling stock?" My answer would be, "Same-customer sales."

Wall Street analysts deserve credit for closely studying same-store sales in retail. But even there, financial analysts can't be sure if they are seeing improved sales with fully engaged customers or through tricky marketing and merchandising that compensates for customer defections — in other words, through what is actually a replacement strategy. It's impossible to see if a company is achieving true organic growth.

The key to organic growth is how your organization performs one customer at a time. And here are the million-dollar questions: Are you developing fully engaged relationships with every single customer? Is your company a partner with every customer, or are you just a vendor? Consider your answers carefully, because the sum total of these relationships is your stock price.

Organic growth is revealed by figuring out how many of your customers have an "advice" relationship with your organization versus how many have a "price" relationship. The ratio of advice to price is key to your company's future. The higher the ratio, the better — and as this ratio moves, so does sales growth. This ratio is your company's best predictor of whether it is creating sustainable growth — or is riding the razorblade.

When it comes to managing customer relationships, many Fortune 1000 companies' offenses come in the form of extremely well-run marketing sales and merchandising practices. And practices such as Six Sigma, lean management, and enterprise relationship management have all been brilliantly used to create leak-proof defenses. But none of these strategies or tactics will help your business go from "good to great," as the popular book says, or even from lousy to good. What these approaches are missing is the magic of sustainable stock increase through a sustainable customer strategy. That is exactly why companies need a genuine organic growth strategy — one that is about moving from price to advice.

The challenge of extreme competition

Now, it's crucial to note that advice-versus-price relationships are present in *all* businesses, organizations, and professions. Advice-versus-price exists in hair salons just as it does in major technology or medical or government sales. Whether the business is dance lessons, pharmaceuticals, new and used cars, jet shares, real estate, hotels, hospitality, churches, suits and dresses, or delis, advice-versus-price relationships matter to some degree in every business in which transactions matter.

Regardless of its industry, the worst thing that can happen to your business is for 100% of your customers to base their relationships 100% on price. When this happens, your leadership needs to go from lousy to good in a hurry. Yes, price matters, but in a great organization, price should account for no more than 30% of your relationship with any customer; the other 70% should be based on your advice and ideas.

The obstacle that prevents leadership from moving from a price to an advice relationship is extreme competition, and it is everywhere. Not long ago, many markets had a handful of competitors per industry, all of which conveniently shared the market, and all were profitable. In those days, third place wasn't that far from first. These "convenient monopolies" represented the state of national competitiveness.

An easy example is the old network television industry, where NBC, CBS, and ABC ruled. Being number one was about the same as being number three. All three printed money for 20 years. Network news and big-city network affiliates made a staggering 50% pre-tax profit. Ad slots were always sold out.

Imagine a conversation from those days between Joe, an advertiser, and a network TV salesperson at the 21 Club over martinis and cigarettes. "I'm sorry, Joe, but we're sold out until January, but I can get you some spots on *Gunsmoke*. By the way, the new rate card will be in effect in January, and prices are going up fifteen percent." Joe takes the deal.

Today, many prices have dropped to unimaginable lows. Twenty-five years ago, Gallup paid 30 cents per minute for phone calls. Gallup now pays only 3 cents per minute. Phil and Phil say it will someday go to zero. If someone had said this 25 years ago, during constant rate increases, no one would have believed it. The thought that prices would stop increasing and would actually drop to 3 cents, let alone to nothing, was not something anyone could have imagined.

And if you look at what has happened in Detroit — where all three car companies used to enjoy a well-defined and rich convenient monopoly — automakers now give away the cars at the cost of labor and steel and attempt to make money on the loans. So now in Detroit, the cars are the "free toasters" to entice you to take the loan. Nobody saw that coming. This is what happens when you bet your organization's future on price.

Advice relationships

It's pretty clear that companies must re-order their priorities or they will go broke. Many are going broke now. They must find an alternative to price slashing, and the solution is to create value based on *relationships*.

Now, you might say, "Tell me how relationships can solve this problem." First, let's drill down to make relationships more actionable; let's define an "advice" relationship. In an advice relationship, someone brings you a new idea, teaches you something she has learned about your industry, or offers you a new way to save money or a new process to streamline operations. She might have a sales lead for you; she might connect you with a valuable new partner.

At the core of this kind of relationship lies a tangible business value, like Partner A demonstrated with Phil and Phil. You must know the customer and his business very well and have a passion for it. Above all, the engine driving the relationship must be your *imagination*. An organic growth strategy demands extraordinary creativity and imagination from the people who interact with customers.

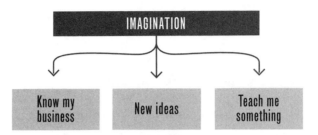

Many consulting firms refer to the highest level of relationship as that of a "trusted advisor." That relationship works in almost any industry. It is not only true for McKinsey, Ernst & Young, and Gallup; it is also true for the wholesale meat salesman.

Doing a great job

Here's a story that illustrates my point. I recently walked to my local bookstore in Georgetown to get the *U.S. News & World Report: America's Best Colleges 2005*. This is a major bookstore, with three stories of books, escalators, a big music department, and a Starbucks coffee shop. I looked all over the store and couldn't find the college report. The staff person I checked with was on the phone to a friend and was ever-so-slightly put off that she was interrupted. "If it wasn't where you looked, we don't have it," she said, then went back to her call. Suddenly, it felt like everyone in the store was unhelpful.

As chance would have it, just as I was getting on the escalator, a real young, super-skinny, 15-year-old-looking kid with a bookstore ID tag asked, "Is there something I can help you find?"

He didn't have the greatest personality in the retail world, and he didn't pretend to. He didn't say, "It's great to have you here." He said, "Can I help you find something?" He not only got wound up helping me find my college guide, but he also found a book that was more precisely what I wanted — a book specifically about law schools. He was grinning because he not only found what I was looking for, but he helped me discover that there was another book that better met my needs.

Then he asked, "Is there anything else I can help you find?" I asked if he was familiar with the book *The United States of Europe*. He said he was, and it was excellent. I told him that I don't like to read hard academic books. He guaranteed me that this wasn't. In the end, I bought two books I didn't intend to buy, and we looked at some others I will soon consider getting as well.

My trip to the bookstore is a perfect example of organic growth. Three outcomes were possible when I walked in the store. The bookstore staff could do a "good" job and sell me exactly what I came for. They could do a "lousy" job and sell me nothing. Or they could do a "great" job by discovering what I really wanted, which was information about law schools, and advising me to buy something I really wanted, something I didn't even know was available — then following up by asking what else I needed and recommending another great idea.

I left the store enthusiastic and feeling victorious about my new books. My clerk was genuinely enthused because I had taken his advice, and we became acquaintances. I will always seek him out on future shopping trips.

One million moments of truth each day

These three potential outcomes not only illustrate the concept of organic growth, but also a phenomenon Gallup calls the "Emotional Economy." For this bookstore, the difference between making $0, $10, or $50 from a customer doesn't lie with its merchandising, its ad agency, or its Six Sigma restocking or shipping techniques; it lies with the sales associate who senses an unmet emotional need and fulfills it. Within the concept of the Emotional Economy lies the potential economic impact of millions of missed transactions — or millions of transactions fulfilled — every day.

As an example, let's say this large bookstore chain has about 1,000 stores, and each day, 1 million prospects walk into them. So every day, there are 1 million moments of truth — 1 million opportunities to provide service that's lousy or good or great.

To dollarize this, let's say the range per transaction is $0 to $50. If 1 million customers were treated like I was by the first clerk, this bookstore chain would go flat broke. They couldn't drop their prices low enough to make sales. If their service was good, they might survive on $10 per transaction. But if the service was great every time, the difference would be $40 on every transaction (the difference between a $10 sale and a $50 sale).

It may not seem like much at first glance, but $40 by 1 million customers is $40 million extra sales dollars every day. Over a year, it adds up to $14 billion, which would triple this chain's current sales and boost their profit 5 to 8 times.

From Lousy to Good to Great at the Bookstore

At the core of every advice-based relationship, there is a tangible business value. For this bookseller, the difference between lousy and good service in one transaction is $10, while the difference between good and great service is $40.

SERVICE LEVEL	RESULT	SALES VALUE
LOUSY	Fail to take the order and sell nothing to a sure prospect.	$0
GOOD	Take an order, and sell the customer exactly what he asks for.	$10
GREAT	Advise the customer to purchase not just what he asks for, but what he really needs.	$50

This may seem like a crazy scenario, but it shows how enormous a company's untapped Emotional Economy can be. The amounts left on the table are huge, especially when a company's customer service is only lousy or good. If this bookstore could improve just 10% of its 1 million daily customer interactions from good to great, it would easily double its market capitalization.

From good to great through organic growth

Many people have asked me, inspired by the popular book, of course, "How can my company go from good to great?" My answer is, "Create organic growth by maximizing the Emotional Economy that exists within your current customer base."

Gallup provides consulting services of various kinds to 100 of the Fortune 500 companies. Only five of these companies are clearly in the great category. I define a "great" company as one that understands the Emotional Economy and has a clear strategy to increase organic growth.

Gallup's research shows that, on average, only 20% of the customers of business-to-consumer organizations are fully engaged; only 12% of the customers of business-to-business organizations are fully engaged.

Is Your Company Engaging Customers?

Businesses that aim to create organic growth must maximize their current customer relationships. Yet Gallup's research shows that, on average, only 20% of the customers of business-to-consumer organizations are fully engaged, while just 12% of the customers of business-to-business organizations are fully engaged.

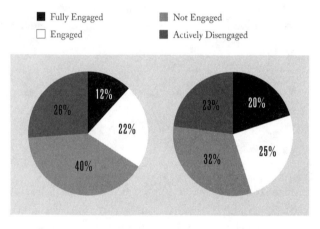

Business-to-Business   Business-to-Consumer

What Wall Street and even the best CFOs still miss is that in business-to-business companies, lousy, good, or great management occurs about one to two years before it shows up as earnings; it shows up more quickly in retail. Basically, earnings are a one- to two-year trailing indicator of customer performance. And a company's success in managing its Emotional Economy is never included in formulas that calculate future earnings. When you maximize this economy, it is called "organic growth."

Right now, there is enormous variation in how companies serve and engage their customers. In the case of the retail bookstore, customer service that ranges from lousy to great means $0 to $50 dollars to this company, 1 million times per day. In the case of Partner A, a successful relationship with Phil and Phil means retaining a growing account.

One more story: I sometimes interview our clients' customers personally to get a feel for their Emotional Economy. During a discussion with the CIO of a large U.S. grocery chain, I asked how he would rate Tech Firm A on a 1-to-5 scale. He said, "a 1, because they do nothing but deliver cheap technology and equipment." I asked who their best supplier of technology was, and he said Tech Firm B. Get this: He said that he would give Tech Firm B his highest marks because rather than just sell him products, "They teach me how to sell more groceries." This CIO spends about 10 times more with Tech Firm B than Tech Firm A.

For most companies, whether they're going from good to great or lousy to good, there is more cash lying on the table here than through any other leadership approach. The newly discovered Emotional Economy that lies within customer interactions is bigger than what W. Edwards Deming found when he first started looking at defects and variation 60 years ago. Remember, Deming discovered that 50% of all U.S. manufacturing costs came from redoing product. The range Gallup finds in customer service performance is as big as or bigger than the defect ranges Deming found in "lousy-to-great" manufacturing.

First steps to institutionalizing organic growth

So how can companies institutionalize organic growth? How do leaders get a large organization deeply focused on a very different customer service strategy, one based more on advice than price? Here are some suggestions:

1. *Measure customer service at the local level, or your employees won't take it seriously.* You must use a short, powerful questionnaire with near-perfect question items that can accurately predict whether an account is in trouble or will grow. Gallup has done this for 20 years, and we've found that separating engaged accounts from accounts that are in trouble is an easy way to predict future buying behavior. Then hold managers and workgroups accountable for their customer performance. Very few companies have succeeded in measuring and managing customer service at the local level, but it's the only way to get everyone focused on customer service. Use this audit as your engine for change.

2. *Make it 100% about money.* First, use your customer service metric to calculate the existing range of performance throughout the company. Just as with Six Sigma, you will find extreme variation in performance

from workgroup to workgroup. Use advanced statistical and economic modeling to show where your company and its divisions could be if they were maximizing organic growth opportunities. Then extrapolate organic growth from the divisions all the way to the company's total market capitalization.

3. *Change compensation and review programs to reflect leader, manager, and employee performance on this highly predictable indicator of organic growth.* Identify teams with fully engaged customers. Make them heroes. Tell everyone in the company their best practices.

4. *Create a website that enables managers to scan "state-of-the-customer" data by division, region, and client teams.* This can become sort of like a global weather map, something that managers check regularly, like stock prices or baseball scores.

5. *Create an organic growth leadership camp.* Replace your current leadership development program with one focused 100% on organic growth. Use this program to teach your managers, salespeople, and key employees how to earn "5s" rather than "1s" from their clients. Help them understand what makes your customer relationships grow and what makes them wither away. Teach them that a price-based relationship fails to create organic growth and that an advice-based relationship is 30% price and 70% advice. Give certifications — like the Black Belt in Six Sigma — to those who master the new approach. These certifications will become the talk of the company because your leaders will learn that there is more money to be made in growing your current customer relationships than in any other growth strategy.

WHO'S DRIVING INNOVATION AT YOUR COMPANY?

by Jerry Krueger and Emily Killham

September 14, 2006

Is innovation important? Over the past several years, business articles and research studies have stressed its significance in creating long-lasting competitive advantage and achieving dramatic increases in organizational performance. In the February 2006 issue of *Harvard Business Review*, author Gary Hamel writes that internal business process and management innovations over the past century "have created more competitive advantage than anything that came from a lab or focus group."

A recent survey of more than 750 CEOs showed that business leaders agree with Hamel's thinking. This study by IBM Consulting Services revealed that company leaders are increasingly focused on innovation as a key mechanism for driving growth. CEOs said they were looking for creative business models and new ideas in products, services, and markets. The CEOs also emphasized the need to look outside the company — including among business partners and customers, the top source of new ideas — as well as inside the company for innovations.

In other words, when it comes to innovation, business leaders aren't necessarily looking to traditional sources, like research and development departments, to contribute big new ideas; they're counting on ideas from their employees, customers, and partners to help drive the organization forward. And engaged employees are most likely to contribute those innovations, according to a recent *Gallup Management Journal* (*GMJ*) study.

Encouraging creative ideas

GMJ surveyed U.S. employees to discover what effect employee engagement may have on team-level innovation and customer service delivery. Gallup researchers studied employee responses to several items about innovation in the workplace to see which factors differed most strongly among engaged employees (29% of respondents) and those who were not engaged (56%) or actively disengaged (15%). (See "The Three Types of Employees" in the Appendix.)

Gallup research has shown that engaged employees are more productive, profitable, safer, create stronger customer relationships, and stay longer with their company than less engaged employees. This latest research indicates that workplace engagement is also a powerful factor in catalyzing "outside-the-box" thinking to improve management and business processes as well as customer service.

When *GMJ* researchers surveyed U.S. workers, 59% of engaged employees strongly agreed with the statement that their current job "brings out [their] most creative ideas." On the flip side, only 3% of actively disengaged employees strongly agreed that their current job brings out their most creative ideas.

The study also showed that engaged workers were much more likely to react positively to creative ideas offered by fellow team members. When asked to rate their level of agreement with the statement "I feed off the creativity of my colleagues," roughly 6 in 10 engaged employees (61%) strongly agreed, while only about 1 in 10 actively disengaged employees (9%) gave the same answer. This suggests that higher levels of employee engagement not only increase the likelihood that individual employees will generate new ideas, it also suggests that idea generation among engaged employees can be amplified when it occurs in a team setting.

GMJ researchers also explored the role that workplace friendships play in promoting innovation. About three-fourths of engaged employees (76%) strongly agreed with the statement "I have a friend at work who I share new ideas with." On the other hand, only 2 in 10 actively disengaged employees (21%) strongly agreed that they have a friend at work with whom they share new ideas. Clearly, friendships do play a significant role among engaged employees when it comes to setting the stage for idea creation and refinement.

The results also suggest that there are significant differences in how engaged and actively disengaged employees view their company's encouragement and acceptance of innovative ideas. Only 4% of actively disengaged employees strongly agreed with the statement "My company encourages new ideas that defy conventional wisdom," while more than half of engaged employees (55%) strongly agreed that their company encouraged such ideas.

Innovation and customer service

GMJ researchers also investigated the effect of employee engagement on customer service innovation. Nearly 9 in 10 engaged employees (89%) strongly agreed that "At work, I know where to go with an idea to improve customer service," contrasted with only 16% of actively disengaged employees.

Engaged employees also involved customers in the innovation and improvement process. When asked to rate their level of agreement with the statement "At work, we give our customers new ideas," 74% of engaged employees strongly agreed that they shared new ideas with customers, contrasted with just 13% of actively disengaged employees.

Gallup's employee engagement research has consistently shown a connection between employee engagement and customer engagement. One factor that can influence customer engagement is an employee's willingness to change — or to "learn and grow" — to meet the customers' changing needs. When Gallup asked workers to rate the statement "I have grown in my ability to positively affect our customers," the results were telling. Almost 9 in 10 engaged employees (85%) strongly agreed that they have grown in their ability to positively affect their company's customers, while only 2 in 10 actively disengaged employees (19%) strongly agreed.

Finally, more than half of all engaged employees (51%) strongly agreed with the statement "At work, my coworkers always do what is right for our customers." This was in stark contrast to the actively disengaged employees: Only 1 in 10 strongly agreed that their coworkers always do what is right for their customers.

Gallup's research into the relationship between employee engagement and innovation strongly indicates that engaged employees are far more likely to suggest or develop creative ways to improve management or business processes. They're also far more likely to find creative ways to solve customer problems or to involve their customers in creating service innovations. Company leaders who want to drive growth through innovation should first create an environment that welcomes new ideas — and should make engaging employees a key component of that strategy.

Results of these surveys are based on nationally representative samples of about 1,000 employed adults aged 18 and older. Interviews were conducted by Gallup by telephone quarterly from October 2000–October 2002, then semi-annually thereafter. For results based on samples of this size, one can say with 95% confidence that the error attributable to sampling and other random effects could be plus or minus three percentage points. For findings based on subgroups, the sampling error would be greater.

INVESTORS, TAKE NOTE: ENGAGEMENT BOOSTS EARNINGS

by Bryant Ott

June 14, 2007

When deciding where to put their money, do investors take into account the engagement level of a company's employees? If not, it's time they did. Gallup research has found that higher workplace engagement predicts higher earnings per share among publicly traded businesses.

When compared with industry competitors at the company level, organizations with more than four engaged employees for every one actively disengaged employee saw 2.6 times more growth in earnings per share than did organizations with a ratio of slightly less than one engaged worker for every one actively disengaged employee.

Of course, not every investor who feels secure putting his or her money in a publicly traded stalwart of the financial banking industry would also buy into an up-and-coming biotech company, and vice versa. That's because no two industries are exactly the same. So to control for fluctuating circumstances particular to specific industries, Gallup scientists controlled the study at the company level. The results show that in addition to growing faster than below-average-engagement organizations, earnings per share for top-quartile organizations outpaced earnings per share for their competitors by 18% during the study period.

Effect on returns

Gallup has studied employee engagement — employees' involvement in and enthusiasm for their work — and its effect on individual and organizational workplace performance outcomes, such as customer advocacy, productivity, profitability, turnover, absenteeism, safety, and inventory shrinkage — for more than 40 years. To study the impact of engagement on companies' share prices, Gallup researchers conducted an exhaustive exploration of both the workplace engagement database and comparable publicly traded competitors to control for variables at the company level throughout different industries. Jim Asplund, Gallup's chief scientist of strengths-based development, sifted through the resources to develop an accurate representation of publicly traded organizations and their financial data during the baseline and study timelines.

"The first task was determining which companies from the database we could get public financial data about," says Asplund, coauthor of a book on employee and customer engagement, *Human Sigma: Managing the Employee-Customer Encounter*. He was able to identify about 90 organizations that were publicly traded in an exchange somewhere in the world and that also met the following criteria, which Gallup devised to ensure an accurate study:

- The entire organization must have conducted a Q^{12} employee engagement survey. This criterion was necessary for Gallup to make accurate comparisons at the company level.

- Public financial data must have been available for each company for the years covered by the research, including the baseline (2001-2003) and study (2004-2005) timelines.

Once researchers had identified the organizations in the employee engagement database that met these criteria, they determined which of their competitors had comparable public data available in each industry and which of those industry peers to include in the study. "A lot of the process involved accounting; we had to track down the relevant financial data and also find the right set of comparable companies to include in the survey," Asplund says.

One way to control for the variability in differing industries is to compare each company to its competition. "Also, earnings per share can really bounce around. So we looked at patterns across time for the organizations in our study," says Jim Harter, Gallup's chief scientist for workplace engagement and wellbeing. "By combining similar companies and coupling their data across a longer period of time, we can better understand the true patterns across highly engaged and less engaged organizations."

The frequency of Q^{12} survey administrations and the amount of experience organizations have with Gallup's workplace engagement practice also affect results. Top-quartile companies averaged nearly three administrations of the Q^{12} survey, compared with an average of just slightly more than one Q^{12} survey administration by the below-average companies. However, even with fewer administrations of the survey, earnings per share for below-average companies rose from the baseline measurement (2001-2003) to 2004-2005.

Beyond return on investment

This research doesn't show investors and business leaders exactly what organizations are doing on a day-to-day basis to develop engaged employees, but the findings do draw connections to a highly visible outcome. In addition to demonstrating differences in overall performance *between* companies, Gallup's meta-analyses present strong evidence that highly engaged workgroups *within* companies outperform groups with lower employee engagement levels, and the recent findings reinforce these conclusions at the workgroup level.

The meta-analysis study shows that top-quartile business units have 12% higher customer advocacy, 18% higher productivity, and 12% higher profitability than bottom-quartile business units. Conversely, bottom-quartile business units experience 31% to 51% more employee turnover, 51% more inventory shrinkage, and 62% more accidents than those in the top quartile of workplace engagement.

"These aggregated patterns show that engaged employees are more likely to stay with their organizations, are less likely to steal or experience accidents on the job, and are more likely to please customers and be highly productive," says Harter, who coauthored a book on employee engagement, *12: The Elements of Great Managing*. "It all adds up to higher profitability, which over time, influences earnings per share."

This research into earnings per share provides powerful proof that employee engagement correlates to crucial business outcomes. Not all shareholders or prospective investors are able to study the culture of the companies they are investing in. That's why this company-level information is a valuable communication tool for company leaders to provide to shareholders and other business leaders.

"I think this study will have a definite impact in reinforcing the importance of studying employee engagement," Asplund says. "The linkage between engagement and earnings per share is more meaningful to some people in an organization than some of the other linkages Gallup can show them, because investor earnings are something that executives really worry about." Harter adds that while the findings don't necessarily describe the daily, specific actions a company takes to increase engagement, the findings do emphasize how important those actions are — and how companies can substantially improve crucial business outcomes by investing in an engaged workplace.

A MILITARY GENERAL'S LEADERSHIP LESSONS

An interview with Lieutenant General Russel Honoré (retired)
by Jennifer Robison

January 8, 2009

You can't blame executives for thinking that leadership must be simpler in the military. In regimented, highly disciplined organizations such as the Army, a leader gives an order, and it's carried out — no dissension, no complaints, no lollygagging. How simple leadership must be for an Army general. Well, let that dream die. People are people in uniform or not, and a leader's job is to get them on track, not simply to bark orders. So says a reliable source, retired three-star Lieutenant General Russel L. Honoré.

General Honoré has served all over the world in a variety of capacities: in South Korea as commanding general, 2nd Infantry Division; in Washington, D.C., as the vice director for operations, J-3, The Joint Staff; as the deputy commanding general and assistant commandant at the U.S. Army Infantry Center and U.S. Army Infantry School in Fort Benning, Georgia; and as the commander of the Standing Joint Force Headquarters — Homeland Security, U.S. Northern Command; among many others.

You may remember General Honoré as the man who coordinated the U.S. military's relief efforts after Hurricanes Katrina and Rita ravaged the Gulf Coast. He's also the author of *Survival: How a Culture of Preparedness Can Save You and Your Family from Disasters*. General Honoré knows quite a lot about bossing people. And he stresses that above all, you shouldn't boss people. A leader's job is strategic: to set people on the right path and "to do the planning and then to motivate the execution," as he says.

As General Honoré relates in this interview, leaders should keep dissenters close because they'll provide a valuable perspective. Leaders should understand the difference between leadership and management so they don't get caught up doing what they're *not* there to do. And if leaders forget any of this, consider geese. Oddly enough, geese offer a valuable lesson about leadership in the real world.

Gallup Management Journal: In the military, people do things because they're ordered to — they can't refuse or negotiate. Yet you've said that human nature and behavior affects the accomplishment of missions. So what role does leadership play when people must do what they're told?

Gen. Honoré: Leadership means forming a team and working toward common objectives that are tied to time, metrics, and resources. The purpose of the commander and the staff is to do the planning and then to motivate the execution. Now, many times you hear leaders say, "This is what we're going to do," but the plans fail if they don't track the execution.

In the military, as in any organization, giving the order might be the easiest part. Execution is the real game. The hierarchy starts with the leadership, which provides vision, wisdom, and motivation. Then there's management. That's turning time, task, and purpose into action. Leadership is working with goals and vision; management is working with objectives. Objectives, as you know, are specific, and they're tied to time, coordination, and resources.

But management is not the same thing as administration; people who do administration work off of checklists. Management works in collaboration with leadership and administration to ensure all the functions of the organization — from personnel to logistics to finance to human resources — are tied together to execute that vision and the goals. Administrators are the people who say, "You gotta fill out a form 5988 if you want to get these assets." Administration ensures compliance. The leader's role is to provide the strategic vision for the organization.

GMJ: "Strategic vision" sounds a bit vague.

Gen. Honoré: In the civilian world, the word *strategy* often means "big things that might happen." In the military world, it means "the purpose of what we're doing, the task to be accomplished, when it will be done, and how and by whom." The purpose is what counts, followed by the tasks and who will do them, how they're going to get done, and when.

That's grand strategy that has been documented over hundreds of years of military operation.

Now what continues to change over time is the advantage technology gives us in executing vision. But technology does not replace the core elements: the role of the leader, the role of management, and the role of administrators.

GMJ: It's not unusual for leaders to get caught up in the management part.

Gen. Honoré: Well, that's very easy to do.

GMJ: Why is that?

Gen. Honoré: In a normal organizational construct, people usually grow from management to leadership, and they have a tendency to do what they know best. So if you were formerly a financial guru but now you're the leader, you probably will spend a little bit more time watching finance. And if, when you were in finance, you didn't always like what those guys in research and development did, you take a calculator and you go in there and do a little micromanaging.

In my case, I was always fond of logistics, even though I was an infantry officer. So I would drive all my organizations crazy about logistics because logistics was always the hardest thing to get done. So many times units failed, not because they weren't capable but because they didn't get the gas, the boots, and the bullets on time.

There's an old saying in the Army that if logistics was easy, it'd be called tactics. *Tactics* comes from a Greek word that means "the arrangement." And what do leaders do? Work the arrangement. They arrange what must be done, and they approve how it will be done. The big thing in industry is always to be the industry lead, because he who sees first, understands first, and he who acts first gets the competitive edge first. That's why the arrangement is so important.

GMJ: What do you do when people buck the arrangement? How do you motivate them to do what they don't want to do?

Gen. Honoré: There's a construct for that. You've got three groups of people in your organization. First, you've got the people who, when you say it, will get it done. Those are the people who want to replace you.

Then you've got the people who are on the team but aren't necessarily motivated to get the task done. Those people are in the middle. You can't run the organization without them, so you take them as they are. They are committed to the company, they're committed to the unit, but they don't work with the enthusiasm of that first group.

And then you have the third group. They're very effective, but they don't seem motivated. They argue with you. What you must decide is, is it OK to have a person from the third group on the team, or should you get rid of him? Members of that third group can be very competent, and many leaders let them go because they aren't jumping up and down every time the boss walks in.

So an art of leadership is to sort those three groups out. You don't have to worry about the ones who want your job. They're clapping every time the boss says something, and they're willing to do whatever it takes to be on the team and be solid key players. Then you've got those who don't cheer, but they get it done. But the third group could be the most productive, because sometimes the least conformist member of that group can say, "Yeah, this is what the boss says, but this is what the organization needs." Some of your best innovation may come from the mavericks.

GMJ: But the last group can cause a lot of trouble.

Gen. Honoré: Yes, but remember that the first group can get you into trouble with "group think." When you're the boss, you might say, "Let's get on with it," which is good for the organization. But then you have a manager from the third group who says, "Yeah, but the boss is wrong." You've got to keep a line of communication open to the leader of that third group because he'll be the one who keeps you out of group think. You can jump on the train awfully quick with an underdeveloped strategy if all you hear is [agreement with] what you just said.

That first group always echoes the leader's words — if the leader says, "It's Miller time!" the first group all says at once, "It's Miller time!" Group two will nod their heads. Group three says, "No, it's Bud time." All three groups give balance to an organization.

This is a pluralistic view of an organization. Group one is good for accomplishing a mission, but if you don't have people bringing up the negatives, you won't have any perspective.

GMJ: Then how do you gain the right perspective? How do you see things like your customers do?

Gen. Honoré: Look at it this way: In the 1960s and 1970s, executives at the major carmakers never drove a car more than six or seven months. When they drove it to work in Detroit when it was thirty degrees below zero outside, they parked it in the executive garage. Then they'd drive it home and put it in the garage at night. Well, people who bought those cars didn't necessarily have the same perspective. The car executives thought that '65 Impala was a great car, but they never had to start it in the cold. They didn't know how their product really performed. I think American industry has lost perspective about their products.

Instead, leaders must be involved with and live with what they're doing. If you're an airline executive and all you do is ride in business class, you'll have a different perspective than that guy sitting back there in the 34th row. But guess who makes the money for the airline? You might have ten people up there in business class, and meanwhile, 150 people are sitting in the back. You need to understand their perspective.

GMJ: What should leaders do when they realize they've made a mistake? Conversely, how can they tell if they're right?

Gen. Honoré: That's where you must rely on your management team to create the right metrics and to keep a keen eye on what your competitors are doing. In the Army, we used to say, "Are we getting the effect we want against the enemy?" In the business world, the saying is "Are we getting the effects from our energy here?" If you're not measuring your results, then you could lose opportunities. People who are very successful will turn problems into opportunities.

Now, assuming you have earned a position of leadership and that it hasn't been granted to you, you will have learned the art of listening to bad news and diverse opinions. Good leaders understand there will be people who will be open and honest with them. Those people may not be right, but they'll bring a different perspective.

GMJ: *How do you create an environment that encourages people to be honest with you?*

Gen. Honoré: When I'm talking to young officers about leadership, I use the analogy of watching geese.

GMJ: *Geese?*

Gen. Honoré: Yeah, geese. They say, "General, what in the hell is that?" I ask them if they've ever noticed that when geese fly, they fly in a V formation. Why do you reckon they do that? It's because they get more flying power from flying in the draft of the lead goose. Geese have learned that the lead goose's job is to go as fast as he can, so the geese in the back all quack as loud as they can to tell the lead goose to go faster.

The other thing you'll find is that when the lead goose gets tired, he'll drop back, and another goose will take charge. And the other geese are still quacking to encourage the new leader to go faster! Faster! Faster!

So if you're the CEO, listen to the crowd behind you. That's the power of getting everybody to go the same direction simultaneously.

WHEN CAMPBELL WAS IN THE SOUP

An interview with Campbell CEO Douglas R. Conant
by Jennifer Robison

March 4, 2010

Douglas R. Conant likes a challenge. The president and CEO of the Campbell Soup Company, Conant picked up the reins nine years ago when the company's share price was down and customer loyalty was on the wane. He knew that he could assemble a team to revitalize the company, revamp the product line, fuel innovation, win back customers, and make Wall Street love soup (and cookies and spaghetti sauce and juice) again.

And engaging the workforce was integral to Conant's plan. Engagement, he believes, creates trust and inspiration — and trusting, inspired employees can accomplish extraordinary things. But he knew it would be difficult work. In fact, he predicted that it would take a decade to get the company firing on all cylinders again and the workforce engaged top to bottom.

And Conant was right — his strategy boosted engagement, productivity, and profitability, just as he'd expected. But before he could take a victory lap, the recession hit. In 2008, consumer packaged goods median shareholder returns dropped 25%. But as Conant says, tough times motivate and energize both him and his team at Campbell. Furthermore, as he explains in this interview, as the economy worsened, Campbell was prepared. The workforce was highly productive, innovation was bubbling, and leadership was tightly focused on winning in the workplace so Campbell could win in the marketplace.

This long process was not effortless, though. As Conant notes in this discussion, at the outset, it required assuaging Wall Street's impatience, pushing an unpopular program through a resistant workforce, and rescuing an unhealthy company — in other words, overcoming a series of difficult challenges. Read on to discover how Conant and Campbell turned those problems into a remarkable success.

Gallup Management Journal: In your first 18 months on the job, you replaced 300 of your top 350 leaders.

Douglas R. Conant: Yes, and it took about another year to get all the right people in the right seats on the bus.

GMJ: About the same time, an initial assessment of employee engagement at Campbell found that the company's scores were among the lowest of any Fortune 500 company Gallup had ever studied. Soon, though, your engagement program started showing results. What was the result of a more engaged leadership team?

Conant: The team became self-governing. As people get engaged, they get engaged in more than just their departments. They start getting engaged in the enterprise, and they have conversations with each other about how the company can move forward, not about how IT moves forward or how supply chain moves forward or how Pepperidge Farm [one of Campbell's subsidiaries] moves forward. When you're engaged in trying to do something special to lift the entire company up, all of a sudden the conversations change. People feel more accountable to each other, and they don't want to let each other down.

It actually gets easier to lead, because the flywheel starts to work. As in the Jim Collins' model, it's simple. Collins says the good-to-great model must have three things. You need disciplined people, which requires getting the right people on the bus. You need disciplined thought, which is how you will compete, and we built the strategy to do that. Then you need disciplined action.

Once you get everybody on the same page and they're all thinking about the enterprise, all of a sudden, the actions naturally become more aligned, and you become more effective in the marketplace. Then people feel even better about it. Then they want to talk to each other more. Then they want to work together more. That's the flywheel effect.

We've gotten to a point where higher executive engagement has brought a focus to the enterprise, not just to pieces of it. That just didn't exist before. My challenge now is to keep the flywheel going, to keep engagement up throughout the entire company, to make sure we have the right people on the bus, and to make sure that, at a high level, the strategy is right.

GMJ: These evolutions take time, and it's hard to explain to Wall Street — which thinks quarter to quarter — that you need two or three years to make substantive changes.

Conant: Well, you can't talk your way out of something you behaved your way into. This is a very mature industry. If you're a wounded company, the other companies that have been around for a hundred years will smell it, and they will take advantage of you in a heartbeat. It takes a long time to get back in fighting form. Jim Collins said it takes seven years to take a company from good to great. He said it would probably take us ten years to go from bad to great, because it takes three years to get the right people on the bus in the right seats. And he was right — there are absolutely no shortcuts.

Before I took the job, I told the search committee, "It took years to get into this; it's going to take us years to get out." We talked about the need to create a three-year set of expectations about how we would get the company heading in the right direction again. I thought we could do it in less time, but it did take about a decade. I told the search committee, "Look, we will improve every year, but let's be realistic: We're starting out uncompetitive every day right now. At the end of three years, we will be competitive on a good day. You can take that to the bank, and we will improve every year on all the key measures."

We communicated our three-year transformation plan to Wall Street. We set the expectations to a reasonable level. And we said, "We'll grow off this base every year." We have grown every year now for nine years.

GMJ: And now you're facing the worst economic downturn in many years.

Conant: That's just the nature of the beast. That's the challenge — but that's what makes it exciting. That's why you need to be more engaged *now*. Now is the time to lift yourself up and take advantage of the strength you've created. Then get out there and do better than all these people who are saying, "Woe is me. It's a tough world. What am I going to do?"

This recession provides a unique opportunity to seize the day, leverage the momentum we're building both in the marketplace and the workplace, and do something really special. My mindset, and I would argue it's the mindset of most of the people in this company, is that we devote more of our waking hours to our work than anything we do, oftentimes more than to our families. If we can't make that work special — meaningful in some compelling way so that we get excited about doing something special — shame on us. Why are we devoting so much time to it? Just to earn a paycheck? That's just not enough. For me and many others at Campbell, it's about leaving a legacy.

GMJ: How do you keep engagement levels up?

Conant: You have to model the behavior; you have to be the change that you want from the company. I write a ton of personal, handwritten notes to people every day. I'm more visible. A few years ago, we started a CEO institute for some of our top leaders, and I'm very involved in mentoring. I'm actively involved in advocating diversity and inclusion work. So I'm modeling the kind of behavior that I want people to bring to the workplace.

Ultimately, you have to do the work. We measure engagement every year, and then managers meet with their teams to create action plans to improve on their results. While our managers play a critical role in building engaged teams, we know that every employee demonstrates leadership by actively taking part in their team's engagement planning. Action planning is essential for us to continuously improve our engagement levels.

GMJ: Do you think that focusing on engagement now will make Campbell a stronger company when the economy improves?

Conant: I'm hopeful, but you never take engagement for granted. I'm always worried about what's lurking around the next corner. We actually had a big blip with our global leadership team one year; their engagement dropped. When we did the work around it, we understood why.

GMJ: That's scary.

Conant: No, it was a gift. We learned what was not working, and we were able to remedy it and go forward. I think if we do this kind of thing right, we'll be even better positioned for the future as a result.

But you know, I'm not afraid of making mistakes. The one thing you must have in this work is humility. You have to talk about mistakes and then talk about what you have learned and how to move forward. You acknowledge missteps right away, you deal with them, and you move ahead. If you don't bring a lot of humility to this work, you lose credibility.

Bill George [former CEO of Medtronic and author of *Authentic Leadership* and *True North*] is a man who did amazing things. He's also a guy who will own a mistake in a nanosecond and say, "Yeah, I made a mistake. How can we work together to fix it?" I think that's a big part of being an effective leader, because organizations can sniff out a lack of accountability. They know you made the mistake, so who are you kidding? Acknowledge it. Customers know too.

GMJ: Campbell has been around for 140 years. Over that time, it has built up many traditions, which is great — but it can also make a company hidebound. Did you have trouble inserting a systemized plan for engagement? Or was the culture ready to accept it as much as you were ready to start?

Conant: The company wasn't ready to do this when I got here. But, you know, we didn't really have a choice. People felt as if we were on death's doorstep, and everything they had tried wasn't working. When I got here, I'm sure they thought that the engagement program wasn't going to work either and that I wasn't going to last. So the organization wasn't initially responsive to my plan. But you just have to keep working the territory and keep pushing as far as the organization is capable of going. You have to bring fierce resolve to the work. As a result of that resolve, engagement is embedded into our culture. For me, there simply is no other way.

THE REAL WAY TO REFORM HEALTHCARE

An interview with Gallup COO Jane Miller and Gallup CFO Jim Krieger by Bryant Ott

March 10, 2010

The ongoing public debate about the nation's healthcare system is leaving everyone involved exhausted and anxious. But the problem of rising costs persists, and it is bound to get worse.

In 2009, the United States spent more than $2 trillion on healthcare, a figure equal to almost 16% of the nation's gross domestic product. About half of these costs are privately funded. Although Congress has tried to reengineer the healthcare industry in the United States, businesses are responsible for paying a large portion of the country's rising healthcare costs.

Companies can't afford to wait around while government and industry leaders debate various plans to reduce healthcare costs. And they don't have to, according to Gallup's chief operating officer, Jane Miller, and chief financial officer, Jim Krieger. Organizations have plenty of options at their disposal to stem rising healthcare costs and instill healthier lifestyles for their workforces right now.

Miller and Krieger are able to demonstrate how creating a company culture of wellness and consumer-driven healthcare can reduce the cost of care while helping employees live healthier, wealthier lives. Consumer-driven care plans and programs place cost and prevention responsibilities and freedoms on the shoulders of employees instead of employers. Companies can take steps to cultivate behaviors that improve individuals' health while decreasing health-related costs for the consumer and the company. This includes investing the necessary time, energy, financial resources, and emotional support to help employees take complete control of their wellness and healthcare costs.

How are Miller and Krieger so sure of this solution? Because at a time when other companies and individuals are paying more for insurance and care, Gallup is creating savings. In this interview, they discuss prudent decisions, unwavering commitment, a clear strategy for creating and sustaining a culture of responsibility for one's health and wellness, and responsible cost awareness and consciousness as the reasons for Gallup's successful consumer-driven healthcare practices.

Gallup Management Journal: How long has Gallup embraced consumer-driven healthcare? What kind of investment has Gallup made in this effort?

Jane Miller: Gallup has stressed consumer-driven care, wellness strategies, and health education transparency since 2000. That year, the leaders of our organization devised and implemented a six-year plan aimed at reducing healthcare costs for the company and our employees. It was during that same period that Gallup created a robust culture of healthy living and preventative wellness throughout the organization.

Jim Krieger: After the first two years of these efforts, our medical premium rate inflation decreased from 21% and 20% in 2002 and 2003 to just 8% in 2004 — seven percentage points lower than healthcare inflation trends nationwide. Since then, our annual healthcare cost inflation has averaged just over 2%. That's unheard of on such a consistent basis, based on our conversations with other companies.

GMJ: Why is this considered so exceptional? What sort of return on investment has Gallup realized?

Krieger: Because while comparable annual healthcare cost inflation across the country remained anywhere between 11% and 15% between 2002 and the present, over the last four years of our six-year effort, annual savings have ranged from 8.5% to 12.5% from Mercer Management's annual Health Cost Inflation reports, for a four-year annual average of 10.02%.

Our program participants realize more than half the savings in lower premium rates, and the company saves the other half while continuing to enhance free preventative health options — all during a time when organizations and individuals are looking to save as much money as possible wherever they can.

GMJ: So how did the company create this culture of consumer-driven healthcare? How did employee behavior play a role in this strategy?

Miller: Cultivating a culture of consumer-driven healthcare seems like hard work, and it is. But the rewards are worth the effort, both for companies and employees.

The top levels of a company's leadership must avidly empower individuals to take control of their health and wellness. This includes helping them understand the costs associated with their health and their lifestyles. Organizations must offer clear and complete communication about ways employees can be more cost-conscious of their behaviors and decisions relative to wellness. And these actions and efforts must be genuine. For Gallup — and for other companies that are enacting strategies similar to ours — transforming individuals' behaviors relative to their health is the only way companies and individuals can take control of rising healthcare costs.

GMJ: In other words, if you can appeal to the emotional side of employees' decision making, you can drive home the importance of embracing ownership for their own health and wellness as a way to save on healthcare costs.

Miller: Exactly. Employees must be emotionally invested in their health and in their decisions as an owner of their healthcare costs. Successfully transforming employees' behaviors relies on a company's ability to effectively frame the importance of health and cost-conscious decisions in an emotional way instead of simply communicating the relative value of such choices.

The key to convincing employees of the benefits of this type of plan is explaining outcomes in ways that emotionally resonate with them. This includes helping employees embrace healthy lifestyles and understand the effects of their decisions. By taking an approach based on behavioral economics, organizations can realize real healthcare change and truly enhance the health of their workforces.

GMJ: What tactics has Gallup used to successfully frame consumer-driven healthcare in its workforce? What works?

Krieger: The major focus of our efforts to reform healthcare is on the cost of care. We tend to believe that if employees are responsible for a greater amount of their out-of-pocket costs, they will understand it is in their best physical *and* financial interest to focus on preventing the most costly chronic diseases and health problems. We offer our employees several medical insurance plans, each of which includes high deductible requirements and allows for health savings accounts and health reimbursement accounts. These accounts allow our employees to decide how much they want to save and how much they want to spend on care.

When we raised deductibles and copays, we hosted company-wide education sessions to show employees a multiyear road map of where we were taking these two shared costs. We took the time to explain the reasons why and the details about the supporting contributions to health savings accounts. We did all this in an effort to move the decision-making power to the individuals and support the first-dollar costs.

By giving them these choices, we feel we are empowering employees to take control of their health and wellness. And the company saves money.

GMJ: But what does Gallup do with the money it saves? Where does it focus those funds?

Krieger: Gallup raised deductibles and copays for plan members, but not drastically all at once. It was more of a steady rise. But we also contribute money to the health savings accounts and reimbursement accounts, and we have added free or near-free proactive and preventative care opportunities at the same time. We invested 100% of our savings and shifted costs right back into the consumer-driven care plans to support preventative measures and allow employees to make their own decisions based on their own needs using the money in their accounts. We committed to the education and the tools and the leadership support necessary to change employees' behaviors.

GMJ: What are some of the efforts Gallup implements to help employees embrace preventative care?

Miller: The amount of money Americans could save in treatment expenses and improved productivity by preventing cases of chronic diseases such as cancer, heart disease, and hypertension reaches into the trillions. The investment Gallup and other companies can make to help employees understand and take responsibility for health prevention pales in comparison to this sizeable sum. That's one of the reasons our company employs the Healthways program, which provides specialized, comprehensive solutions to help people improve their health and reduce care costs.

As Jim mentioned, we give employees financial incentives to join the program. In return, they receive annual biometric health screenings; health risk assessments; personal health reports; and access to lifestyle management resources, coaching, and other tools and materials that provide exercise and nutritional information.

GMJ: Do those exercise and nutrition resources actually prevent health issues and improve wellness?

Miller: Yes. In addition to the resources provided through Healthways, we can attribute our healthier workforce partly to employing full-time professional personal trainers. Their job is simply to ensure a high level of healthy living for any Gallup associate who wants help. We've seen individual employees lose up to 80 pounds, drop more than 75% of their body fat percentage, and transform from couch potatoes to competitive athletes. We provide our employees with these resources because they keep people healthy and prevent avoidable diseases.

GMJ: But Gallup isn't the first company to figure out that exercise and proper preventative care will improve wellness while cutting care costs. What makes these results different? What's the secret?

Miller: There is no secret — that's the frustrating part. It's similar to explaining why fad diets are exactly that — fads. There is no substitute for a healthy lifestyle. Plenty of other organizations share the same types of success we have with our consumer-driven care efforts. And it doesn't matter how large their workforces are or how much money they generate in revenue. There seems to be an endless number of ideas and plans companies can implement to help employees improve their health and wellness while cutting care costs.

GMJ: You mentioned that other organizations have similar initiatives to promote wellness and reduce healthcare costs. Can you give some examples?

Miller: Two organizations with strategies similar to ours have a strong corporate presence in Omaha, Nebraska, where Gallup's worldwide operational headquarters is located. We've learned a lot from Union Pacific Corporation, one of the country's leading transportation companies, and from Alegent Health, a 120-year-old faith-based healthcare provider in Nebraska and southwest Iowa, when it comes to consumer-driven care options.

Union Pacific, which employs 45,000 people, counts among its organizational goals to be the healthiest workforce in America. Why? One reason is safety: They know that people who are more focused on their job and who are generally healthier are going to be safer. Their internal and external studies show health and wellness factors such as weight, stress, depression, and fatigue highly correlate with safety incidences.

So Union Pacific built a fitness facility in its headquarters building in 1988. But that didn't help the employees who called any section of the company's 32,000 miles of railroad track the office, so the company struck deals with more than 600 fitness centers across the country where employees can show their identification and work out free of charge. The company also offers employees the HealthTrack program, a health risk assessment and wellness improvement program targeting ten risk factors such as inactivity, excess weight, and smoking.

The leadership at Alegent Health believes the best and fastest way to improve value and address broader issues within the healthcare industry is to give consumers more information and greater control over how they spend their healthcare dollars. Like Gallup, Alegent offers employees tools, access, and incentives to improve their wellness and care cost savings, including health savings accounts and health reimbursement accounts in addition to PPO insurance options. Alegent offers preventative care free of charge and constantly reminds employees of the positive outcomes relative to focusing on health prevention. This includes measuring participants' wellness efforts and health outcomes using health risk assessments and other surveys.

GMJ: It sounds like you're saying that real healthcare reform will only come through a critical mass of companies and organizations implementing consumer-driven healthcare plans that pave the way for healthier, more cost-conscious employees.

Miller: From our perspective, the solution to the nation's healthcare cost problems and individual wellness issues won't come from simply shifting the financial burden from one place to another. It lies instead in changing the focus from paying a premium to combat problems to embracing a focus on prevention, wellness, and responsibility for one's health, one company at a time.

What if, for example, the top one thousand companies in the United States invested the time, effort, and initial investment required to instill the types of cultures and improvements highlighted in the previous examples? What would the cost/benefit calculation look like? How much money could these companies save in providing consumer-driven healthcare options to their employees? How much money could these employees save if they were healthier? How much improvement would they see in their quality of life? And perhaps most important, by how much could these efforts limit the occurrence of costly chronic diseases throughout these companies' workforces?

We believe companies of all sizes can implement consumer-driven care plans. Organizations can change the healthcare climate themselves, one workforce at a time. It takes commitment from leaders who truly care about the health and wellness of their employees. It takes clear communication with and education for employees about how to make healthy behavioral choices — and why to make these decisions. And it takes the right framing and explanation of how employees can save money and provide themselves a healthier quality of life by participating in consumer-driven healthcare.

Our company is just one organization, just one employer. The key to extrapolating the successes achieved by companies such as Gallup, Union Pacific, and Alegent Health is getting other leading organizations — regardless of size or industry — to step forward, embrace similar strategies, and implement a culture of consumer-driven healthcare. That's when one company becomes one hundred, and then one thousand, and then ten thousand. And that's when things will really change.

THE BUSINESS CASE FOR WELLBEING

by Jennifer Robison

June 9, 2010

Many organizations think that employee wellbeing is, well, none of their business. And there's some sense to that — wellbeing does seem ill-defined, private, and ultimately unmanageable. According to Tom Rath, leader of Gallup's workplace research and leadership consulting practice, and Jim Harter, Gallup's chief scientist for workplace management and wellbeing, it's not. But wellbeing *is* gravely misunderstood.

Rath, Harter, and teams of Gallup researchers spent years studying wellbeing to find out what it is and how to increase it. They surveyed people in more than 150 countries; partnered with leading economists, psychologists, sociologists, and physicians; and conducted and studied in-depth wellbeing research. Ultimately, as Rath and Harter wrote in their *New York Times* and *Wall Street Journal* bestseller *Wellbeing: The Five Essential Elements* — wellbeing is the fulfillment of five distinct factors.

Rath and Harter discovered these core dimensions to be "universal and interconnected elements of wellbeing, or how we think about and experience our lives." When those factors are fully realized, people thrive — and so do businesses.

In the U.S., the average sick day costs a business about $348 in lost productivity, according to the Bureau of Labor Statistics and a study published in 2003 in the *Journal of Occupational and Environmental Medicine*. When we adjust this number because people are sick on weekends and non-working days and because some work does get done on sick days, the cost is still approximately $200 per sick day. But people with high levels of wellbeing get sick less often; as a result, they cost their organizations less.

The Five Essential Elements of Wellbeing

For more than 50 years, Gallup scientists have been exploring the demands of a life well-lived. More recently, in partnership with leading economists, psychologists, and other acclaimed scientists, Gallup has uncovered the common elements of wellbeing that transcend countries and cultures. This research revealed the universal elements of wellbeing that differentiate a thriving life from one spent suffering. They represent five broad categories that are essential to most people:

Career Wellbeing: how you occupy your time — or simply liking what you do every day

Social Wellbeing: having strong relationships and love in your life

Financial Wellbeing: effectively managing your economic life

Physical Wellbeing: having good health and enough energy to get things done on a daily basis

Community Wellbeing: the sense of engagement you have with the area where you live

Among the most "suffering" employees — those with the lowest wellbeing scores — the annual per-person cost of lost productivity due to sick days is $28,800. For workers who are at the midpoint of the "struggling" zone, the cost is $6,168. But for employees with the highest levels of wellbeing — those with the highest scores in the "thriving" category — the cost of lost productivity is only $840 a year.

Another recent study compared the disease burden — or the incidence of high blood pressure, high cholesterol, heart disease, back pain, diabetes, depression/anxiety, and sleep apnea/insomnia — of 662 people with varying levels of wellbeing. For each disease, Gallup entered the average annual cost into its database — and after adjusting for demographic differences — found that respondents in the thriving category averaged $4,929 per person annually in disease burden cost versus $6,763 a year for respondents in the struggling and suffering categories. That's a 37% per-person cost differential. In other words, for an organization with 1,000 workers, thriving employees cost their employers $1.8 million *less* every year.

And if that weren't startling enough, Gallup tracked changes in disease burden from 2008 to 2009 for the same group of 662 people. Gallup studied the relationship between wellbeing and recent changes in disease burden and found that the average annual new disease burden cost for people who are thriving is $723, compared with $1,488 for those who are struggling or suffering.

Clearly, it's in an organization's best interest to keep its employees healthy. But wellbeing is comprised of five interrelated elements. Pushing one dimension of wellbeing at the expense of the other elements won't improve wellbeing very much. To reap the most benefits from thriving employees, organizations should pay attention to all five elements.

Career and engagement

Career Wellbeing is a natural place to begin — and it might be the best place to start too. "Most people don't realize how closely intertwined their Career Wellbeing is with their overall evaluation of their life and daily experiences," says Harter. "Our research suggests that this may be the single most important element of one's wellbeing."

Career Wellbeing doesn't necessarily refer to paid work. Rath and Harter note that stay-at-home parents and devoted volunteers can have high levels of Career Wellbeing. But to be engaging, work does have to provide "interest and purpose and the chance to use your strengths regularly," as Harter says. "We spend more of our waking hours at work than anywhere else, so work really needs to provide that outlet." That's why, Rath and Harter suggest, it's a seminal element of wellbeing. And that might also be why they found a strong connection between employee engagement and wellbeing. Engaged employees have a sense of purpose and get to do what they do best every day.

Whether or not engaged employees have high levels of wellbeing — though it's realistic to expect that engagement naturally promotes wellbeing — these workers are an organization's best asset. Workgroups with many engaged employees realize substantially higher levels of customer engagement, productivity, and profitability compared to teams with less engaged employees. And engaged teams have less absenteeism, lower turnover, fewer accidents on the job, less theft or unaccounted for merchandise, and fewer quality defects.

Engaged employees who are thriving in Career Wellbeing are twice as likely as actively disengaged employees to be thriving in their lives overall. In contrast, people in disengaged workgroups are nearly twice as likely to be diagnosed with depression, have higher stress levels, and are at greater risk for heart disease. And perhaps not coincidentally, engaged employees are 21% more likely than actively disengaged employees to get involved in a wellness program offered by their employers. This relationship between engagement at work and involvement in wellness programs is consistent across body mass index (BMI) groups (normal, overweight, and obese) and people with and without disease burden. In other words, even among people who are classified as obese and those who have pre-existing disease burden, those with higher Career Wellbeing are more likely to become involved in wellness programs that are offered.

There are many ways organizations can improve Career Wellbeing. Leaders and managers can help employees connect their work to a higher purpose and focus on employee strengths, which can reduce active disengagement. Even simple but powerful motivational techniques, such as recognition for goal achievement, go a long way toward enhancing Career Wellbeing.

Socializing is good for business

While considering the performance boost inherent in higher Career Wellbeing, employers should also think about employees' Social Wellbeing. Even though socializing may sound antithetical to workplace productivity, Gallup found that socializing at work is actually good for business. "Among those with thriving Social Wellbeing," says Rath, "49% were thriving in their careers." Moreover, Gallup has found that employees who say they have a best friend at work are seven times more likely to be engaged in their work. Those who don't feel that way have a mere 1 in 12 chance of being engaged. Yet only 5% of workers strongly agree that their organization helps them build stronger personal relationships.

Nevertheless, it can still be galling for managers to watch employees chatting around the coffee pot when they should be working. The research, however, indicates that office chit-chat serves a productive purpose. "We cite an interesting finding in the book that came from a team at MIT," says Harter. "They studied people who were just walking around different office settings and found that the social cohesiveness created by conversations that weren't at all work-related actually helped boost workplace productivity."

Furthermore, Gallup's research shows that to have a thriving day, people need six hours of social time. Few organizations would condone six hours of surfing Facebook on the company dime, but employers can promote Social Wellbeing *and* organizational goals through social activities — such as mentoring programs and development opportunities — that can produce important business results.

The money issue

It's logical to assume that organizations are central to employees' Financial Wellbeing — employers issue paychecks, after all, and people rely on those paychecks to meet their needs. But Financial Wellbeing is more about financial security than monetary compensation. In fact, Gallup's studies show that financial security has nearly three times the impact of income alone on employees' overall wellbeing.

That's why pay itself doesn't necessarily correlate to engagement or wellbeing — and neither do pay raises. However, if employees don't "perceive their pay to be fair and equitable," says Rath, "it can lead to disengagement and cause them to leave when a better job comes along." There's also the impact of financial worries on employees' mental and physical health. Low Financial Wellbeing can lead to stress, anxiety, insomnia, headaches, and depression. And those are costly problems.

Ironically, most organizations don't seem to promote their employees' Financial Wellbeing very well. Only 6% of employees strongly agree that their organization does things to help them manage their finances more effectively. But business might be uniquely — perhaps perfectly — situated to improve employees' Financial Wellbeing. Financial security is integral to wellbeing, and most organizations offer investment, profit sharing, or savings opportunities.

One way organizations can improve their employees' Financial Wellbeing is to make the default setting of savings programs opt-out rather than opt-in. For example, most employees won't participate in a retirement plan if they have to consciously opt in. But when the default is for employees to be automatically enrolled, more than 80% participate in the retirement plan.

Furthermore, according to Rath and Harter, spending money on experiences or on others does more to increase people's Financial Wellbeing than spending on things or on themselves. "With experiences, you get a lot of value. There's the anticipation of the experience beforehand, for months beforehand sometimes," says Rath. "Then you get the actual experience itself. And then you usually have fond memories of the experience afterward." For that reason, it might be wise to encourage workers to use their vacation time for actual vacations.

Physical effects

Clearly, doing things like encouraging vacations offers psychic benefits. But Physical Wellbeing matters too. As insurance costs have increased, many organizations have made efforts toward improving health in the workplace, and that's wise. Those efforts will be even more effective, however, if the organization reinforces healthy behaviors by making healthy choices easy and unhealthy choices hard. Gallup found that only 9% of U.S. employees say it is very easy to find healthy food at their workplace, and fewer than 5% say their organizations offer financial incentives for leading a healthier lifestyle.

While many leaders focus on the direct costs associated with paying for their employees' medical care — such as prescription drugs, doctor visits, hospital stays, and insurance premiums — employees with low Physical Wellbeing could be taking an even larger economic toll. When someone with struggling Physical Wellbeing shows up for work, it is highly unlikely that he or she has the energy to achieve as much as an employee with thriving Physical Wellbeing can. And employees with high Physical Wellbeing simply have more energy and get more done in less time. They are also more likely to be in a good mood, thus boosting the engagement of their colleagues and customers.

Offering incentives for lowered cholesterol and providing more vegetables in the cafeteria is a good place to start. But subtler changes can help too — and can be as simple as designing workspace layouts so people have to walk a little farther every day, sponsoring workgroup athletic events, or hiring a chef for a monthly demonstration of healthy cooking. Organizations can't mandate health, but they can direct employees to changes that outlast the workday.

Community outreach

Organizations can also direct employees to look outward into the larger community. That's because having employees who are thriving in Community Wellbeing improves an organization's image and increases its positive impact on the community. On the other hand, when organizations run their business in isolation, they miss out on potential gains in Community Wellbeing for their employees and organization.

This aspect of wellbeing may be the most familiar to business: Organizational leaders have a long history of service in their communities, and many organizations actively support local philanthropic projects — and sometimes their employees' chosen charities as well. When organizations invest in employees, employees contribute more to their communities. In one study, Gallup found that people in the most engaged workgroups (those in the top quartile of Gallup's employee engagement database) were 56% more likely to give money to the community, and they gave 2.6 times more money than people on less engaged teams (those in the bottom quartile).

Corporate support for community initiatives can result in positive customer relations and recruiting outcomes. Such behaviors can also improve employee wellbeing by creating the opportunity for social connections and local involvement.

Improving wellbeing

Some organizations offer health promotion programs. Others actively encourage giving back to the community through donating time or money. And a few take a hand in encouraging employee Financial Wellbeing. But for the most part, the crucial activities that promote wellbeing are left to employees.

Because employee wellbeing has such a large impact on organizational wellbeing, businesses would be wise to measure and manage it. Fortunately, many organizations do have programs in place that affect wellbeing. But the wellbeing factor — if it's recognized at all — isn't leveraged as well as it could be. Businesses that manage wellbeing consciously, consistently, and with an eye toward improving key outcomes are more likely to have a profound influence on organizational and employee wellbeing.

THE PRICE OF POOR WELLBEING

by Bryant Ott

August 12, 2010

There just might be something to the saying "I feel like a million bucks."

OK, the monetary amount is probably an exaggeration, but Gallup researchers Jim Harter, Ph.D., and Sangeeta Agrawal have determined the price people pay for poor wellbeing, both financially and physically. Those costs extrapolate to the larger discussion of healthcare reform in the United States. And taking the right actions to increase wellbeing can have a significant impact on improving healthcare and lessening the burden of poor wellbeing on employees, their employers, and the country as a whole.

Wreaking havoc, physically and financially

Harter, chief scientist for Gallup's workplace management and wellbeing practices, and Agrawal, a senior researcher, conducted a series of surveys of U.S. households. They measured overall wellbeing and monitored change in disease burden for specific chronic conditions such as high blood pressure, high cholesterol, depression, heart disease, diabetes, sleep disorder/insomnia, and anxiety.

The study defines increase in disease burden as one or more new incidences of the previously mentioned conditions. Increases in disease burden were identified using three independent surveys that measured whether respondents were diagnosed with one or more new conditions in 2009 compared to 2008 or had no new diseases diagnosed in 2009.

Gallup categorizes individuals' overall wellbeing as "thriving" (strong, consistent, and progressing), "struggling" (moderate or inconsistent), or "suffering" (at high risk). One-third of struggling or suffering adults (35%) reported an increase in their disease burden. Comparatively, one in five thriving adults (21%) reported an increase in disease burden. This means that adults with struggling or suffering wellbeing were 64% more likely than adults with thriving wellbeing to have one or more new disease conditions diagnosed in the past year.

Along with the physical cost, that 64% figure is significant because of the financial costs associated with these conditions. Gallup's researchers reported a distinct difference in the cost of disease burden when comparing these two groups of adults. Thriving adults averaged an annual disease burden cost of $4,929 per person compared to $6,763 per person averaged by struggling and suffering adults. This represents a 37% cost difference, with struggling and suffering adults averaging $1,834 more in disease burden costs per person than their thriving counterparts.

Those assessments include all diseases, not just new incidences from the previous year. Still, the news is grim for those who are struggling or suffering. From 2008 to 2009, the average annual cost of new disease burden for adults who were struggling or suffering was $1,488 per person; this was about twice as much as the $723 in average annual costs of new disease burden incurred by thriving adults.

Gallup researchers also measure wellbeing in five dimensions of an individual's life: Career, Social, Financial, Physical, and Community. Harter and Agrawal found that the likelihood of disease burden increase is lowest for adults with thriving levels of wellbeing in all five dimensions. And as the number of dimensions in which an adult is thriving decreases, the likelihood of disease burden escalates. Individuals who were not thriving in any of the five dimensions of wellbeing, for example, had a 35% likelihood of incurring increased disease burden in the previous year compared to 11% for those with thriving wellbeing in all five dimensions.

Not surprisingly, the total annual disease burden costs and new disease burden costs increase as the number of wellbeing dimensions in which individuals are thriving decreases. In 2009, the annual cost of disease burden for individuals who were not thriving in any dimension of wellbeing was $7,393 per person. In sharp contrast, the cost was $2,976 per person for people who were thriving in all five dimensions — a 60% difference. Similarly, the per-person cost of change in disease burden resulting from a new diagnosis was $1,842 for people who were not thriving in any wellbeing dimension but just $195 for those who were thriving in all five dimensions (a difference of 89%).

Thriving Wellbeing Is Good for Your Health

The likelihood of increased disease burden was lowest for adults with thriving levels of wellbeing in all five dimensions — Career, Social, Financial, Physical, and Community. As the number of dimensions in which adults are thriving increases, the likelihood of new disease burden decreases.

■ % Likelihood of Disease Burden Increase in the Past Year
by Number of Dimensions Thriving

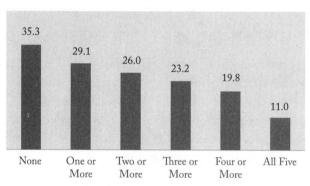

| None | One or More | Two or More | Three or More | Four or More | All Five |

Adjusted for demographic differences

Chronic economic impact

The macroeconomic costs of poor wellbeing are astonishing, yet unfortunately consistent. A 2007 Milken Institute report titled *An Unhealthy America: The Economic Burden of Chronic Disease* estimates that seven of the most common chronic diseases cost the economy more than $1 trillion each year. The Centers for Disease Control (CDC) and Prevention finds that chronic diseases such as asthma, heart disease, cancer, and diabetes kill more than 1.7 million Americans each year and are responsible for more than 70% of the deaths in the United States. The CDC observes that to a large degree, chronic illnesses like the ones included in Gallup's research are preventable and the result of the daily choices people make, and about 133 million Americans live with at least one chronic condition. Further, one in four of these adults experience significant limitations to their daily activities. All told, the financial implications of chronic illnesses are enormous, with a majority of the money spent on healthcare due directly to these types of diseases.

What does this mean for the nation's employers? Gallup's research shows that adults with thriving wellbeing are less likely to suffer an increase in disease burden and the related financial consequences. The outcomes of higher wellbeing can translate to savings in healthcare costs for individuals and employers; they can also reduce absenteeism among employees and limit what the Milken study refers to as "presenteeism," or showing up for work to avoid losing wages but working below par. The Milken study finds the long-term impact of chronic diseases on economic growth more substantial than treatment costs and lost labor outputs.

How organizations can remedy problems

It would make sense, then, for employers in all industries and sectors to focus on helping workers improve their wellbeing. Physical Wellbeing is obviously a large part of the equation: Milken's 2007 study found that lowering obesity rates could reduce illness, significantly lower the national healthcare treatment bill, and improve GDP. What's at stake? Hundreds of billions of dollars of improvements in productivity and total economic impact, not to mention reduced mortality rates. But Gallup's wellbeing science emphasizes the importance of the other four dimensions: Career, Social, Financial, and Community Wellbeing.

"A high percentage of healthcare costs are due to things we can all directly affect — our diet, exercise, weight, and other habits," says Harter, who coauthored the book *Wellbeing: The Five Essential Elements*. But many other aspects of our lives can influence our long-term physical health, including our careers, social lives, finances, and communities.

"Most people have the right long-term goals of good health; engaging careers; positive relationships; financial security; and having a safe, engaging place to live," says Harter. "The problem is that people don't always align short-term incentives with these longer term goals — that is, to do things that make them feel better today and give them a better life in the long term."

Harter says that employers are well-positioned to help people improve their short-term and long-term wellbeing in all dimensions. "Probably the most efficient place to create change in this area is through organizations. They have natural social networks, cultural expectations, and an infrastructure to provide wellbeing resources. Through ongoing measurement, education, and positive defaults, employers can take the lead in creating awareness and long-term change," Harter says.

But what specifically can employers do to improve their workforce's wellbeing? Harter believes it starts with building an engaging work environment. This includes fortifying an organization with great managers and offering employees support and structure to achieve thriving levels of wellbeing in all dimensions. "While organizations probably shouldn't approach wellbeing from a paternalistic perspective," says Harter, "they can offer opportunities that improve the odds that their employees will do what is best for themselves and make clear that thriving wellbeing is an expectation within the organization."

Because employees *and* employers pay the financial consequences of poor wellbeing — and healthy employees often foot the bill for their unhealthy colleagues — it makes sense to invest time and money in providing resources to help employees improve all dimensions of their wellbeing. Harter says organizations can do things to enhance their employees' social lives by giving them opportunities at work to build relationships and the flexibility to take care of family matters when necessary. He believes that organizations can offer employees options to learn financial management skills through relevant programs and education classes. And he thinks organizations can take an active role in connecting employees to community involvement opportunities that fit their strengths and interests.

"Over time, the brand of an organization can be that employees expect their lives to be better in five years as a result of working for that organization," Harter says. "Organizations have already accomplished this with employee engagement, and the next logical extension is employee wellbeing."

"It's important that organizations work on prevention and early intervention by understanding that the wellbeing elements are interdependent," Harter says. "Prevention doesn't just involve motivating people to take part in exercise programs and make healthy food choices. It involves thinking about how these good habits interact with all the other wellbeing elements. As with engagement, the most progressive organizations will realize that their job is to improve people's lives as they improve their performance."

These survey findings come from a database featuring a longitudinal sample of 662 adults compiled by combining three independent surveys from the Gallup Panel of U.S. households. Two of the surveys took place in 2008, and the third took place in 2009. The research controlled for age, marital status, income level, gender, and education level. Estimates of disease burden cost for each disease were adjusted to 2009 healthcare, absence, and short-term disability costs and calculated to find the total cost of disease burden and the total cost of disease burden change.

LEADING ENGAGEMENT FROM THE TOP
by Jennifer Robison

November 2, 2010

"You'd be amazed at how much I don't know about my business," says Tim, who owns a large construction company in the Midwest. "I know everything about the financials, the strategy, and the industry. But I don't know exactly what my frontline guys are doing, and I barely know what their supervisors are doing. I don't even know the office gossip, because no one tells that stuff to the boss."

Tim worries that crucial items are escaping his attention, but he knows that if he spends more time on nitty-gritty details, he'll have less time to run the company. He suspects that visibility is useful, but he doesn't know if watching someone nail 2x4s promotes overall strategy. And though he says he works very closely with the company's top leaders, he's certain that the construction supervisors are fundamental to the company's success.

"The best I can do is figure out how things went based on the numbers that come in," Tim says. "By then, it's too late to change things."

Energy pattern
Tim is right to suspect that his crew supervisors are driving performance indicators, because they play a key role in engaging or disengaging his frontline staff. But according to research recently conducted by Sangeeta Agrawal, a Gallup consultant, and Jim Harter, Ph.D., Gallup's chief scientist of workplace management and wellbeing, so do Tim's middle managers, his executive team, and Tim himself.

Workplace engagement is the core of the unwritten social contract between employers and employees. It also serves as a leading indicator of financial performance. That's vital for leaders like Tim who otherwise must depend on backward-looking indicators like pre-tax profit, overtime rate, and waste minimization.

Agrawal and Harter assembled data on 190 organizations from Gallup's employee engagement database. All had conducted Gallup's employee engagement assessment, the Q^{12}, at least twice. On average, each company had 4,477 employees, of whom 92 were executives, 597 were middle managers, and 3,788 were frontline workers.

What Agrawal and Harter were looking for was a pathway for engagement. Employee engagement can be considered a kind of energy. It causes known reactions, and it requires a source. But what they wanted to investigate was: How does this energy move? Does engagement radiate, starting from a central point and moving outward in all directions? Or is engagement more like electricity, moving in a one-way path from one starting point to an ending point?

These are important questions, because knowing the answers gives business leaders clues to the best place to start with their engagement initiatives. "Knowing how engagement works gives clarity on where to focus first," says Harter. "Engaging ten thousand people at once can seem impossible. CEOs can't meet with that many people on a continual basis."

With that in mind, Agrawal and Harter tested four hypotheses: whether engagement moves from executives to managers to frontline workers, from executives to managers and the frontline, from the frontline to managers to executives, or from managers and the frontline to executives. When they'd finished scrutinizing the numbers, they were left with an unassailable conclusion: The engagement current runs strongest in one direction, and it starts at the top.

"Engagement comes from leaders. People look to leadership to set the tone and expectations. Leaders make engagement important," says Agrawal. "If executives don't set the stage and practice what they preach about engagement, it'll be harder for others to follow."

The numbers support this. Managers who are directly supervised by highly engaged executive teams (those in the top quartile of employee engagement) are 39% more likely to be engaged than managers who are supervised by executive teams with below-average engagement.

Similarly, frontline employees who are supervised by highly engaged managers are 59% more likely to be engaged than those supervised by managers with below-average engagement.

So it appears there's a "mediation effect," as social scientists call it, in which executives affect managers and managers affect frontline employees. This is good news for leaders like Tim who wonder where their time is best spent. It's best spent with the people they see most often anyway. "You should focus your efforts locally," says Harter. "Work on engaging the team around you, and engagement will cascade."

The path to engagement

Agrawal and Harter were interested in knowing more than the energy flow of engagement. They also wanted to know which transmission pathways were strongest or if they were all equally effective. To investigate, they performed a "path analysis" for each of the 12 elements of employee engagement. (See "The 12 Elements of Great Managing" in the Appendix.)

The analysis showed that different items had different effects on different kinds of workers. For instance, the strongest pathways from executives to middle managers are the elements related to: learn and grow, mission or purpose, progress, and opportunity to do best. The strongest pathways from middle management to the front line, on the other hand, are:

- best friend
- knowing what's expected
- materials and equipment
- opportunity to do best
- mission or purpose
- recognition

To influence the front line through the mediation effect, executives should concentrate on these items:

- mission or purpose
- opportunity to do best
- materials and equipment
- learn and grow
- best friend

And to push engagement through the whole organization — the only way they really can radiate rather than cascade energy — executives should focus on the elements related to: mission or purpose, knowing what's expected, and progress.

Agrawal and Harter caution that every one of the 12 engagement items is important, and none should be overlooked. They further believe that this cascade effect works regardless of the size of the company. "This pattern emerged across the different sized companies we studied, although the cascade effect is less relevant in very small companies where the CEO can have direct contact and influence on employees more regularly," says Harter. "Engagement in very small companies is higher, probably due to ownership and autonomy. As organizations grow, engagement needs to be maintained across levels, and it starts at the top."

Friends in high places

That begs one obvious question: From what source do executives draw their engagement? According to Barry Conchie, coauthor of *Strengths Based Leadership: Great Leaders, Teams, and Why People Follow*, CEOs and other high-ranking leaders need a particular kind of talent to be "engageable." "CEOs create the conditions for their own engagement. They can influence all the pieces," says Conchie. "If a CEO is disengaged, he or she is either unfit for the role or incapable of creating engagement."

Still, a significant part of employee engagement is related to human interaction. "That's why the board relationship is critical," says Conchie. "Taking time to make the right changes and additions to the board can provide an effective counterbalance and level of accountability for a CEO. These aren't always the safest relationships for CEOs to cultivate, but they can be an important antidote to the loneliness that many CEOs express feeling; they also can help counter a sense of social isolation that might hinder CEOs from taking positive steps to boost their own engagement."

But those aren't the only people a CEO needs around. Agrawal suspects that highly engaged CEOs have a core group of mentors and peers — people these leaders can turn to who understand them and who will push them when they need to be pushed. "There's a lesson here: When people reach a high status, they may forget they still need to learn and grow and develop," Agrawal says.

It's important for leaders to spend time with other leaders. They need to be engaged and to engage — and not just for their own sake. Their engagement is crucial because it sets the tone for the engagement of everyone in the company. Engagement is too valuable to neglect at any level in the workplace.

As Tim puts it, "I probably don't need to know how many nails an hour my guys put in. What I need to know is how many they *could* put in if they wanted to — and what makes them want to."

MANAGING CHANGE

YOUR JOB MAY BE KILLING YOU

An interview with Gallup workplace expert Jim Harter
by Jennifer Robison

April 13, 2006

The high cost of health insurance has prodded many American businesses to use creative strategies to encourage healthier habits among employees, from on-campus gyms and weight-loss programs to healthy food in the cafeteria; some businesses even employ on-site nurses.

But wellness programs can't be mandated, nor can good health. There's only so much an organization can do to promote healthy habits among employees. Furthermore, it's an uphill battle: As workers age, they become more expensive to insure and treat. But recent research suggests that business may be overlooking an important cause of ill health and high insurance costs: workplace stress.

We all know that stress can be hard on one's health, but recent research suggests it can actually be deadly. Jim Harter, Ph.D., Gallup's chief scientist of workplace management and wellbeing, has been studying wellbeing and the workplace for the past 20 years, and some of the recent research on the workplace and health has astonished even him. One finding that has grabbed his attention: Workplace stress apparently can be linked to heart disease — the number-one cause of death in American men and women over 35 — in a large proportion of workers. Worse yet, heart disease in these employees is separate from other health factors, such as weight, diet, smoking, or family history.

Considering the billions of dollars business invests in health insurance and the negative impact on revenue from lost productivity and absenteeism due to employee illness, reducing stress should be a crucial focus for any organization. Dr. Harter thinks that there's an often-overlooked answer: workplace engagement. He bases his theory on what Gallup research has uncovered about the connection between the quality of the workplace and stress and what scientists are learning about stress and illness. In this interview, Dr. Harter discusses the connection between health, engagement, and profitability — and what managers can do to increase all three. Read on — it'll do your heart good.

Gallup Management Journal: What effect does physical wellbeing have on psychological wellbeing in the workplace?

Dr. Harter: Well, there have been a few studies on that, and researchers are finding that there's a significant interaction between work stress and health. In other words, if people are in an ongoing work situation that is negative or stressful, they have a higher potential for negative health consequences.

There's still a lot of work to do to understand the connection between work stress and health problems. That's why we need to dig into it and study it in more depth, so we can help organizations understand why doing what you do every day has an effect on worker health.

We already know that engagement is related to organizational outcomes like profitability and workgroup productivity, retention, and absenteeism — all of which have an impact on the bottom line of an organization. So understanding the linkages between wellbeing, health, and engagement is particularly important. I think we could understand that at an even more granular level as we learn more about psychobiology.

GMJ: So what are the relationships between health, stress, and engagement?

Dr. Harter: Scientists in our field are finding very substantial relationships. People who are engaged in their work have much lower self-reported stress than those who are disengaged.

A recent study in Germany, reported in *Psychosomatic Medicine*, for example, suggests that cortisol levels are higher among people with high self-reported levels of stress at work in comparison to people with lower self-reported stress. Cortisol, which is secreted by the adrenal glands, is a hormone necessary for the functioning of almost every one of our body parts. It's released in response to physical or psychological stress. Too much or too little leads to a variety of physical health symptoms and disease states. Extreme stress causes higher than needed levels of cortisol to be released.

Studying cortisol levels in the body is one way scientists can objectively measure stress and its consequences to one's physiology. In particular, the research in Germany revealed connections between chronic work stress and morning cortisol levels. People with high stress and high levels of cortisol are more likely to miss days of work and will probably be less productive each day.

We also know that people with poor work environments report more stress. If you're not as engaged in your work, you're less likely to be productive, and you're less likely to help the organization achieve the outcomes it wants to achieve. You may be less able to function in a team context.

We don't know yet if stress causes disengagement or if stress is a result of disengagement. There's a lot to study. But research suggests that the quality of the workplace can have a direct impact on the stress that people feel, which subsequently affects cortisol levels, which could then contribute to health problems like heart disease. It isn't a one-to-one formula, but the workplace and stress seem inseparable. There are many potential ramifications for organizations, including healthcare costs and lost productivity.

GMJ: So how stressed is work making us?

Dr. Harter: In the United States, 30% of the working population reports that there have been three or more days in the last month when the stress of work has caused them to behave poorly with family or friends. Among actively disengaged employees, an alarming 54% agreed that work stress had caused them to behave poorly with family or friends, while only 17% of engaged employees reported that stress had caused them to behave poorly. The percentages are similarly high in other countries. [See "The Three Types of Employees" in the Appendix.]

GMJ: What are the linkages between stress, cortisol, and heart disease?

Dr. Harter: There's an interesting study from England that was recently reported in *Archives of Internal Medicine*. Researchers looked at 6,442 men in civil service departments who had no prevalent coronary heart disease at the baseline of the study. The researchers measured various aspects of the work environment directly related to quality of management, including getting criticized unfairly by their boss, getting information from their boss, how often their boss was willing to listen to their problems, and how often they received praise for their work, things like that.

Then they tracked the incidence of coronary heart disease for an average of 8.7 years and found a 30% lower likelihood of coronary heart disease for employees with positive perceptions of their work environment compared to those with unfavorable perceptions of their work environment. The findings remained consistent even when the researchers controlled for age, ethnicity, marital status, educational attainment, socio-economic position, cholesterol level, obesity, hypertension, smoking, alcohol consumption, and physical activity.

This 30% difference in coronary heart disease incidence is just shockingly important when you consider that Gallup research, which covers 4.5 million employees in 112 countries, indicates that fewer than one in every two employees feels strongly that they have a supervisor at work who cares about them as a person. And fewer than one in every three employees feels strongly that they have someone at work who encourages their development.

GMJ: So a major explanation for the 30% difference in who got heart disease was a bad workplace?

Dr. Harter: The research would seem to suggest that. Thirty percent is a much higher percentage than I would have guessed. The questions that people will instinctively ask are: Is the difference just due to the fact that these people have difficult lives in general? Don't they take care of themselves? Are these people just fatalistically flawed in some way? But the researchers actually controlled for the many other known predictors of heart disease. They found that in addition to all these other factors that are typically examined, the workplace environment contributed 30% to the risk of heart disease. That's a lot.

GMJ: How many people are affected by heart disease?

Dr. Harter: According to various sources, every minute, one American dies from a coronary event related to coronary heart disease. Thirteen million Americans have heart disease, and many more are at risk of getting it. And it's expensive to treat: Heart disease costs the American economy billions of dollars a year. And it's the leading cause of death for all Americans 35 and older, men and women.

GMJ: So what control do managers have? What can they do to reduce these risks?

Dr. Harter: They can do a lot to prevent bad stress, the kind that can be a contributing factor to heart disease — or, as the study in England suggests, the kind that can *cause* it in some people. Gallup research has found that managers have direct influence over whether people are praised, whether people feel appreciated, whether people get the information they need to do their jobs. Managers can create environments that facilitate independent thinking and teamwork. These are all factors that managers often control — and even if they don't have direct control over them, they can influence people who do have control of them. So managers control or can influence the factors that create productive employees; they also control or can affect the things that keep employees engaged, lower employees' stress, and can keep health costs down in their companies.

GMJ: Well, that's kind of a God-like position, isn't it?

Dr. Harter: Kind of. We've known that managers are profoundly important in the workplace. For example, when we do research for the first time in an organization, we find wide variation in engagement levels from workgroup to workgroup, and we also find wide variation in productivity from workgroup to workgroup. Some day, I think we'll know how much variation exists on things like cortisol levels and heart disease risk and other factors; this early research indicates that managers may have a direct bearing on that as well. We *do* know that engaged employees have 27% fewer unexcused absences than actively disengaged ones, and that's a big sum in lost salary — salary that isn't turned into productivity in organizations.

GMJ: So what can you do if you think that your manager is giving you a heart attack — literally?

Dr. Harter: Well, you can either realize the importance of the relationship with your manager and confront the issues that are causing stress in your life, or you can get a different manager. You might realize that your relationship with your manager affects things other than just your work. It may affect your health. That may stimulate some people to redefine their relationship with their manager or to find a different manager. In fact, many employees do find another manager: Employee turnover is substantially higher for poor versus good managers.

Organizations need to take the workplace environment and the quality of employee/manager relationships seriously, because the health of employees may have an enormous effect on the bottom line in lost productivity, absenteeism, and insurance costs.

GMJ: What should senior executives do if they know some of the managers under them are creating disengaged employees? It might be difficult to go to the CEO and say, "I think some of our managers are killing people."

Dr. Harter: [*Laughs*] I'm laughing because it's such a strong statement, but it could be true. One of the things we found is that there is a cascade effect in organizations. If you're a manager of managers, your level of engagement has a relationship to the level of engagement of the people you manage, which then has a relationship to the engagement of the people they manage. So if you're a manager of managers, you can set the tone. You can have an effect on whether the culture is positive — whether the culture promotes engagement. Through example, you can show that it's important to praise people when they do good work or that it's important to give people the right tools for the task when you ask them to do something.

As a side note, we found that the Q^{12} item with the highest relationship to stress at work might seem like the most boring of the questions — "I have the materials and equipment I need to do my work right." [The Q^{12} is Gallup's 12-item employee engagement survey.] But if you think about it, that statement provides important clues to employee engagement and employee stress. Think about the last time you were asked to complete an important task, but you weren't given the materials you needed to do the work right. You probably thought something like, "Okay, they asked me to do this job, and I want to do it, but they're not giving me what I need to do it. They're tying my hands." That can cause enormous stress.

So I think that managers of managers can have a direct bearing on promoting employee engagement — and preventing stress — because they're in charge of getting employees what they need and providing other crucial kinds of employee support. How they manage their managers sets an example for how the rest of the organization should function.

GMJ: A lot of companies have wellness programs — gyms and diet programs are two examples. Do you think that programs like these have as much or more impact on health than increasing workplace engagement would? If you have a limited amount of dollars, where do you put them?

Dr. Harter: I think both are important. I can't tell you which has more importance because the research has shown that both are important, and we're still learning about how each one contributes independently, but they interact considerably. Both require that someone take action. I think that there are ways that organizations can encourage people to take care of themselves. There's a lot of potential for creative thinking in this area.

In any case, whether you're a manager in a position to increase engagement in the workforce or an employee who can influence engagement within your own role, you need to take engagement — and stress — seriously. Executives and managers want to help their company reach their financial goals, and many employees do as well. But to tell people that the quality of the workplace may affect their risk of coronary heart disease . . . well. It hits home a little quicker. And that's one area where scientists should focus future research.

Additional Reading

Schlotz, W., Hellhammer, J., Schulz, P., and Stone, A. (2004) "Perceived work overload and chronic worrying predict weekend-weekday differences in the cortisol awakening response." *Psychosomatic Medicine,* 66, 207-214.

Kivimäki, M., Ferrie, J., Brunner, E., Head, J., Shipley, M., Vehtera, J., and Marmot, M. (2005). "Justice at work and reduced risk of coronary heart disease among employees." *Archives of Internal Medicine,* 165, 2245-2251.

CAN MANAGERS ENGAGE UNION EMPLOYEES?

by Steve Crabtree

May 11, 2006

If management takes a more active role in engaging its unionized workers, does that reduce the need for organized labor? Will unions view systematic efforts by management to keep employees happy and fulfilled as an attempt to undermine their own support? If so, how can companies defuse the situation by working *with* unions to support employee engagement?

Executives and managers tackled these and other questions at a recent Gallup roundtable discussion on engaging union employees, which took place in Washington, D.C. The 25 participants came from companies in a variety of industries, but all either had a large proportion of union employees or must account for the influence of unions in their labor market.

Public attitudes toward unions

Jim Harter, Ph.D., Gallup's chief scientist for workplace management and wellbeing, got the event started with a review of recent Gallup data on labor unions. He stated that Americans are less likely to belong to labor unions than they were 50 years ago. In the 1940s and 1950s, about one in six Americans told Gallup pollsters they belonged to a union; today the number is about one in ten. Unions still enjoy public support, although Americans' likelihood to say they approve of them has also declined somewhat in recent decades. Currently, 58% of Americans say they approve of unions, while 33% disapprove. A slight majority, 52%, say they've tended to sympathize with unions in labor disputes over the last two or three years, while 34% say they've sympathized with the companies.

From a manager's perspective, the crucial question is how the presence of a union colors his or her relationships with employees. Gallup's data suggest that union employees are, on average, less engaged than non-union employees. The percentage of actively disengaged employees is considerably higher among unionized than non-unionized employees in the same company. (See "The Three Types of Employees" in the Appendix.)

In some cases, the sizeable differences may be because union employees tend to have different roles within the company than other employees. For example, at a power utility, the electricians may be unionized but not the administrative staff. However, the roundtable participants agreed that union membership itself can contribute to an "us versus them" mentality that can also diminish employees' sense of rapport with their companies. One participant, who said her company's approach was to partner with unions, said that "There are more adversarial relationships in some areas, and those are reflected in our employee engagement scores."

In discussing Gallup's data with roundtable participants, Harter stressed two other points. The first, gleaned from a Gallup Poll of the U.S. working population conducted in October 2005, is that unionized employees are more likely to say they will stay with their companies throughout their careers, but they're slightly less likely to recommend their companies to family and friends as a place to work. In other words, the sense of security their union affiliation gives them may encourage unionized employees to stick around — but that feeling doesn't translate into a greater emotional attachment to their jobs.

The second point is that the relationship between engagement and productivity is equal in union and non-union environments. Gallup's research with companies suggests that it may be harder to engage employees in a union environment, but engagement has just as profound a relationship to productivity in union and non-union environments.

Key insights

The averages notwithstanding, Harter notes there are many unionized workgroups that rank highly in Gallup's database of workplace engagement studies. Though it can be a challenge to build strong emotional connections with unionized employees, many companies do it. The roundtable discussions produced a number of useful insights into how they pull it off:

Make the engagement-building process open, inclusive, and non-threatening. If union employees perceive an employee engagement survey and subsequent impact planning processes as secretive and threatening rather than constructive, the effort is essentially doomed from the start, the roundtable group said. Employees are less likely to provide unbiased responses, and the union is more likely to do whatever it can to keep its members from participating.

When a government agency decided to focus on engaging its frontline employees as part of a broader effort to raise customer satisfaction, one of the first issues it needed to address was to ensure that the process was open and non-threatening. "[The union's] biggest concern was that the surveys not be used to promote a witch hunt," said an analyst attending the roundtable. "They wanted to know it was part of a learning environment, that it was non-threatening." Once that orientation was clearly established, the union threw its weight behind the agency's efforts to improve engagement.

Involve union officials in the survey and resulting change processes. The same government agency went on to win union officials' full support by offering them input in the development process of the employee engagement survey. Beyond the survey's core engagement questions, additional items were negotiated between the agency and the union so both had a stake in the survey's outcome. The survey has been a success, the agency's representative said; the resulting impact plans have boosted employee engagement, and customer satisfaction is slowly but steadily rising.

Several of the roundtable participants also mentioned that it's important to emphasize that the company is not trying to undermine the union's role. Attempts to raise engagement in a union workplace should include close communication with union representatives, and, ideally, their active support is enlisted.

As one participant stated, "That all sounds nice," but union officials are often highly skeptical of, and sometimes downright hostile to, employee surveys of any kind. How can companies overcome that resistance? One manager suggested that safety concerns can be a good initial connecting point. Gallup research shows a strong relationship between employee engagement and workplace safety in a variety of settings. "The relationship between engagement and [workplace] safety is hard to argue with," the manager said. "It's an easy starting place for agreement, which can then flow into other areas."

But participants also sounded a note of caution against allowing the union to hijack the engagement program for the union's own purposes. They underscored the importance of being highly informed about both the union's local and national agenda — and realistic about its politics. Though it's seldom easy, one participant said, managers who understand union leaders' point of view may be able to use employee engagement as a rallying point to build trust between the company, its employees, and the union.

Use action planning to develop new lines of communication with employees. One reason union-management relations can be contentious is that it's hard to get everyone to agree on what's best for workers. Several of the roundtable participants described how their companies have used engagement efforts as opportunities to find new ways to let their employees speak for themselves.

One of the roundtable participants is an executive at a large service-based company in an industry where employee burnout and turnover tend to be very high. Yet the organization maintains high levels of employee engagement and, in fact, has been able to halt several union attempts to organize employees at its facilities. The company's leadership recognizes that employee engagement is particularly critical in their industry, the executive said. Managers conduct regular action planning with all employees to address their facilities' engagement levels.

What's more, executive-level leaders use that action-planning process as an opportunity to meet directly with groups of hourly employees in different locations. The resulting dialogue gives leaders powerful insights and employees a strong sense of connection to the company. As some participants said, being able to voice their opinions about important matters like health benefits and retirement planning can create valuable champions of engagement among frontline managers and employees.

"Listening is important to them," said the service industry executive, "and the outcome is important to us."

Perhaps most importantly, as one participant said, using engagement programs can open up new lines of communication and increase the flow of creative ideas that serve to keep the organization vital. That participant, a manager at a large power utility, described special Intranet sites designed to enable all employees to express their opinions and maintain a dialogue with the company's leadership. "The more engaged groups are submitting more ideas," she said. "And more of those ideas are being implemented. We've found that engagement fosters innovation throughout the organization."

Recognize that unions can help the company increase employee engagement. The presence of labor unions can pose a challenge to companies that intend to raise employee engagement, but it may also present opportunities. When union-management partnerships can come together to focus on aspects of engagement, such as growth and development opportunities, all employees may benefit.

Best of all, the devotion some unions inspire in their members can serve as a model for companies seeking to achieve a similar connection with employees — particularly, as one roundtable participant said, when it comes to communicating a clear, consistent purpose. "People want to belong to something they can believe in," the participant said. "The organization needs to talk about purpose, mission, and values — and then align them with behaviors. That's fundamental to engagement, and historically, unions have done better at that [than businesses]."

WOULD YOU FIRE YOUR BOSS?

by Bryant Ott and Emily Killham

September 13, 2007

Popular media often lampoons the boorish behavior and limited intellect of the stereotypical corporate manager. From the clueless supervisors such as Michael Scott (on NBC's sitcom *The Office*) and Bill Lumbergh (from the cult comedy film *Office Space*) to the pointy-haired boss in the popular comic strip "Dilbert," pop culture is littered with examples of dimwitted directors and belligerent bosses who are often pitted against the protagonist — the modern employee. And though these characterizations are created for punch lines, chances are, most employees have encountered at least one or two bosses like these during their careers.

But what are employees' options? If they were fictional employees at Dunder Mifflin, they could make fun of Scott behind his back. If they worked at Initech, they could try to avoid answering Lumbergh's calls to work over the weekend.

But what would happen if Dilbert could tell his pointy-haired boss exactly what he was thinking in those comic thought bubbles? Would he fire the head honcho? It's likely that the employees managed by Scott and Lumbergh would show their boss the door. But how do the opinions of these pop culture personas compare with those of the actual U.S. workforce? The answer, it turns out, depends on whether employees are engaged in their workplace.

Survey says ...

The *Gallup Management Journal* (*GMJ*) surveyed U.S. employees to discover if employees would fire their boss — and what effect workplace engagement might have on their willingness to give their boss the boot.

Gallup researchers studied employee responses to see which factors differed most strongly among engaged employees (26% of respondents) and those who were not engaged (56%) or actively disengaged (18%). (See "The Three Types of Employees" in the Appendix.)

The results of this poll show that 24% of employees in the United States would fire their boss if given the chance. Not surprisingly, engaged employees aren't the ones wanting to bid their manager farewell. Just 6% of engaged workers say they would fire their boss if they had the chance, while 51% of actively disengaged associates would get rid of their leader if they could.

This finding is consistent with earlier *GMJ* research, which indicates that engaged employees consider their relationship with their manager to be crucial to their success. Of engaged employees, 49% strongly agree that "A strong positive relationship with this person is crucial to my success at work," while just 12% of actively disengaged employees strongly agree with the same statement. In contrast, just 6% of engaged employees strongly disagree with this statement, compared to 33% of actively disengaged employees who strongly disagree with this statement.

Gallup uses its employee engagement survey, the Q^{12}, to measure workplace engagement and glean insights about the kinds of manager behaviors that are most likely to cause employees to disengage from their workplaces. The *GMJ* survey results show that employees who doubt that their manager cares about them as an individual are far more likely to want to oust their boss.

Slightly more than half (53%) of employees who say they would fire their boss if they had the chance disagree with the Q^{12} item "My supervisor, or someone at work, seems to care about me as a person." Conversely, just 8% of workers who wouldn't fire their manager disagree with the "supervisor cares" item. It seems simple enough: If workers feel like their supervisor or someone at their company cares for them, they aren't as likely to want to fire their boss, according to workplace engagement research.

Less likely to recommend their company

Pop culture provides extreme examples of what can happen when employees don't want their boss to supervise them anymore. Gallup research, in contrast, reveals a more subtle impact on business outcomes, but one that can profoundly affect a company's workforce and its sales and service. Workers who would fire their boss, for instance, are more than twice as likely as those who wouldn't dismiss their manager to not agree with the statement "I will be with my company one year from now" (37% versus 17%). Just about 20% of the U.S. workforce overall disagrees with this statement.

So, if employees who want to fire their manager are less likely than others to be working at their company a year from now, who will take their place if they leave? Probably not a friend or family member. Just 11% of workers who would fire their boss would recommend their current company as a great place to work to friends and family; but more than 40% of workers who would not fire their leader would recommend their company as a great place to work. Once again, the answers to this question among those who would not dismiss their boss are closer to those of the overall U.S. workforce (49%).

Employees who want to fire their manager not only won't recommend their company as a place to work to friends and family, they also aren't in a hurry to recommend their company's products and services. Only one-third of these workers (33%) say they would endorse their organization's goods and services. This is a significantly smaller percentage compared to responses to this question from those who would not fire their boss (54%) and the overall U.S. working population (49%).

Employees who want to fire their boss — especially workers who are actively disengaged — aren't likely to burn down the office building. They probably limit their grousing about their boss to their own inner monologues or to quiet exchanges with other employees over cubicle walls. But employees' disengagement with their supervisor can have real — and negative — consequences for their companies.

Results of these surveys are based on nationally representative samples of about 1,000 employed adults aged 18 and older. Interviews were conducted by Gallup by telephone quarterly from October 2000–October 2002, then semi-annually thereafter. For results based on samples of this size, one can say with 95% confidence that the error attributable to sampling and other random effects could be plus or minus three percentage points. For findings based on subgroups, the sampling error would be greater.

THE PROBLEM OF PAY

by Rodd Wagner and Jim Harter
Adapted from 12: The Elements of Great Managing

May 8, 2008

Should anyone have needed proof that the topic of pay induces intense emotions, the Italian government provided it on April 30. For a few hours on that date, Italians were treated to a chance to retrieve online the tax returns of all 40 million of their fellow citizens who paid taxes in 2005. The access was a parting gift from the outgoing government of Prime Minister Romano Prodi. Posting everyone's income was a "simple matter of transparency and democracy," said the departing deputy economy minister who authorized the move.

Italians reacted with a combination of horror that their own data were revealed and eagerness to know what the rich, the famous, and the neighbors were earning — or at least saying they were earning in a system known for rampant tax evasion. The website was clogged with the curious before public outrage shut it down.

Two years earlier, British newspaper columnist Polly Toynbee touched the same live wire when she advocated making all pay public. "People do know more or less what everyone else earns in the public sector, so why not make it compulsory for all?" she argued.

Norway and Finland make tax returns public, she observed. Toynbee cited research finding that fairness and "transparency" are more important than the actual amount of one's salary, so why not — as the column's headline said — "Throw open the books so that we can see what everyone earns." "After the initial shock," she assured her readers, "people would soon get used to the idea."

The day the piece appeared, a blogger wrote to the columnist, asking, "How much do you earn per annum?" She refused to answer the question. "An organisation has to go public all together."

In ways they may not have intended, the Italian government and the British columnist made a crucial point: Pay is complicated. In fact, pay is so thorny that it behaves like none of the 12 Elements of Great Managing, the dozen aspects of the work environment that Gallup's research showed are most important to measure and improve. (See "The 12 Elements of Great Managing" in the Appendix.)

Companies frequently ask why Gallup does not include a compensation statement in its Q^{12} employee engagement assessment. The answer is that while an employee's response to each of the 12 Elements predicts how he will perform in the future, his answer to a pay question is so bundled up in psychological complexities that asking it usually causes more problems than it solves. Pay is a status-laden, envy-inspiring, politically charged monster. Getting it right is crucial, and that begins by not underestimating its hazards or lumping it in with other aspects of an engaging workplace.

In its irrationality, pay is like many of the 12 Elements — ideas that seem logical on the surface, yet are both surprising and exceptionally complex when processed through the human mind. But compensation is much messier than any of the 12 Elements. A number of basic truths about the psychology of pay demonstrate why managers must view their compensation strategies through an emotional lens if they want to maximize how well they motivate workers:

Higher pay does not guarantee greater engagement.

A supervisor might assume going in that the more she pays her team, the happier they will be. But there's a lot of truth to the old saying that "Money doesn't buy happiness." It doesn't necessarily buy engagement either.

One of the sociological puzzles that presented itself in the last few decades is why, if people spend so much of their energy in pursuit of higher incomes, the attainment doesn't bring the hoped-for result. "Increases in our stocks of material goods produce virtually no measurable gains in our psychological or physical wellbeing. Bigger houses and faster cars, it seems, don't make us any happier," wrote

Robert H. Frank in his book *Luxury Fever: Why Money Fails to Satisfy in an Era of Excess.*

Five leading researchers writing in the journal *Science* concluded: "The belief that high income is associated with good mood is widespread but mostly illusory. People with above-average income are relatively satisfied with their lives but are barely happier than others in moment-to-moment experience, tend to be more tense, and do not spend more time in particularly enjoyable activities."

Good and bad employees are equally likely to think they deserve a raise.

Most employees are less than completely satisfied with the pay they are receiving. This should not come as a shock, given people's desire to progress, ability to find things to buy, and awareness of their every sacrifice for their employers. But the real fly in the ointment is that when asked a pay question, the worst performers are not very objective. They are just as likely as the best employees to say they should be paid more. At one company, when employees were allowed to set their own salaries, "it was a disaster: the good workers set them far too low, and the bad ones set them far too high," wrote the company's chief executive.

In posing any question to its associates, a company sets up an expectation that it will do something about the results — an expectation that can backfire if the issue is not addressed. If you ask a friend if he'd like to go to the baseball game with you, he's likely to not just say, "Yes," but also, "When do we leave?" If you ask if someone is happy with her pay, she will likely not just say, "No," but also, "Where's my raise?" Although some employees in almost any company "deserve" an increase in pay, asking every employee his opinion neither identifies who should get a raise nor gives any useful information to company leaders.

Some incentives can backfire, decreasing employee motivation.

When companies slice incentives into too many small pieces, they have the opposite of their intended effect. Paying for a small act communicates to the worker: "You wouldn't normally want to do this, so we're going to pay you to do it." While logically the reward should be a further inducement, it instead decreases motivation. What is meant as a bonus the mind unconsciously takes as a bribe.

"When people are rewarded for doing an interesting activity, they are likely to attribute their behavior to the reward and thus discount their interest in the activity," wrote professors Edward L. Deci, Richard Koestner, and Richard M. Ryan after analyzing 128 studies of how rewards influence behavior.

When children are asked to collect money for a charity, those who receive a higher reward do, in fact, collect more than those who are offered a smaller incentive. But children whose only inducement is the knowledge they are doing something good for someone else collect more than either the high- or low-reward groups.

If a small payment is given to induce more blood donations, the number of people who show up at the blood bank is less than if there is no payment at all. "The stipend turned a noble act of charity into a painful way to make a few dollars, and it wasn't worth it," wrote Steven Levitt and Stephen Dubner in their book *Freakonomics*. In the scientists' terminology, the piecemeal rewards "crowd out" the "intrinsic motivation" of the task itself.

Sales commissions and piecework pay are sometimes the best ways to hold people accountable. Pay-for-performance tactics can help keep workers' eyes on the goal and can even build engagement. But when used as a catch-all strategy, paying for doing can just as often backfire.

Pay is more about status than about paying the bills.

Numerous studies show that a person's satisfaction with his pay is affected more by how much he out-earns those around him than by the absolute level of his pay. Assuming the purchasing power of a dollar is the same in the following two situations, which would you prefer? (A) Your yearly income is $50,000, while others earn $25,000 or (B) Your annual income is $100,000, while others earn $200,000? Given that choice, half the people will choose a lower absolute salary that puts them at the top of the heap.

Columnist Toynbee argued that shining light on everyone's salary would lead to greater equality, "trust and social glue." Several pieces of evidence suggest just the opposite. Publicly traded companies in the United States are already required to report the compensation of their CEOs and the four other highest paid executives in the business. It may be that executive compensation has grown incredibly fast not in spite of the disclosures, but because of them, as corporate leaders fought for position on published lists of the highly compensated.

If the goal of disclosures is restraint of executive pay, "history is not promising," wrote columnist Floyd Norris in *The New York Times*. "The rise in executive pay began after more disclosure was required and bosses could see what others were getting. Their standard of comparison went from what others in the company were getting to what other bosses got. And every boss deemed himself above average."

Pay comparisons among employees spark intense emotions.

People are fascinated by what other people make. Like few other attributes, pay allows the rank ordering of individuals, an unvarnished display of where each stands in the hierarchy. Lists of moneymakers, whether *Forbes'* compilation of the richest people in the world or a local newspaper's list of CEO pay in the market, are always splashed on the cover.

Once a year, *Parade* magazine, the Sunday insert in many U.S. newspapers, publishes a special issue headlined "What People Earn." It shows a sampling of salaries from stars and political leaders to everyday workers, a little financial voyeurism into data usually considered impolite or taboo at a lesser distance. One of the attractions of *Parade*'s version is that, in finding the salaries of ordinary Joes and Janes, the reader can see who makes more or less than he does. It's one of the publication's best-read issues.

When the comparisons are closer to home, such lists change from fascinating reading to potentially explosive information. *The Wall Street Journal* told the story of one woman who found on the office copier a document containing the performance ratings, base compensation, raises, and bonuses for 80 of her colleagues. She was "outraged that a noted screw-up was making $65,000 a year more than more competent colleagues, while some new hires were earning almost $200,000 more than their counterparts with more experience," said the story. "The discovery led her to question why she was working weekends for less pay than others were getting. 'I just couldn't stand the inequity of it,' she said. Three months later she quit."

While individual pay usually should not be public, compensation criteria should be.

Individual pay is usually best kept confidential, but common knowledge of established salary criteria is important to feelings of fairness. Workers need to know, as one study found, "how pay plan goals are established, the pay plan goals themselves, how the plan goals are evaluated, and how the payouts are determined." Only from such widely understood information can the workgroup have a belief in what social scientists call the "procedural and distributive justice" of the system. Without it, the organization is exposed to perceptions of favoritism, opportunism, or discrimination.

A hypothetical *Harvard Business Review* case study lists several of the disparities that can creep in over time: the new hires lured in with more money than veterans make, substantial salary differences between departments, and the higher salaries better negotiators gain over those who agitate less, to name a few. In the entertaining case study, a computer-savvy employee decides to punctuate her departure by e-mailing the salary file to the entire company, creating predictable angst.

The question for decision makers is how large of a riot would be sparked if all pay were public. If a company can honestly say that based on a common knowledge of how it calculates pay, most employees would not find huge surprises in such a leak, the business has this base covered.

WHY HOPE MATTERS NOW

An interview with psychologist Shane Lopez
by Jennifer Robison

June 25, 2009

It's easy to cultivate a sense of doom right now. Economists have to search ever deeper in the past for times as bad as these, and some say things could still take a turn for the worse. There are ample reasons to give up hope.

But business leaders should not abandon hope, says Shane J. Lopez, Ph.D., Gallup senior scientist in residence and research director of the Clifton Strengths School in Omaha, Nebraska. That's because hope serves a fundamental business purpose. Dr. Lopez defines hope as the energy and ideas that drive people to change their circumstances. So without hope, there would be no goals, no motivation, and no improvement. Without hope, work has no point. Hope has the power to make bad times temporary.

That's why it's increasingly important for leaders and managers to understand the significance of hope and to instill it in employees. In this interview, Dr. Lopez discusses the mechanisms of hope, what happens to people who lose it, and what happens to companies that keep it. He explains how managers can help people who are being fired retain their sense of hope. And finally, he explains the ultimate value of hope: It's what's going to help get us out of this mess.

Gallup Management Journal: *This economy has made leaders, managers, and employees fearful. Is that dangerous?*

Dr. Lopez: Many people will make it through [the economic downturn] relatively unscathed in terms of their current positions. Having those folks function in a way that allows an economy to bounce back over time is important. My biggest worry is that if everybody shifts into fear mode, it will stymie innovation and growth in all sectors. Then when the world markets open up a little bit, some leaders will lag behind because they're not ready for change and growth.

GMJ: What good does hope do us now?

Dr. Lopez: In a section on hope in their book *Strengths Based Leadership,* Tom Rath and Barry Conchie wrote about *initiators* versus *responders.* I think folks who have high hope are both responders and initiators. They see problems and obstacles, and they knock them out. That's the responding part of high hope; responders make good things happen in good times and bad. Then there are the folks who are able to step back — in good times and bad — and say, "I'm going to initiate; I'm going to put that big idea on the table and try to move it forward. I'm going to attempt to take us in a new direction. I'm looking to create something out of nothing." Those folks will be the ones who will be standing tall in two or three years when things begin to bounce back in a significant way.

Hope keeps us in the game. With low hope, we stop interacting with the world. We pull back. Literally, we don't show up. We just move through life in a zombie-like state. We all go through periods of sustained low hope, and they don't lead to anything good at all. But hope for the future — maybe even the distant future — is what keeps people focused and moving in a direction that makes sense for their welfare and the welfare of an organization.

GMJ: When things are bad, how can managers sustain hope? How can they keep their people moving forward in spite of the gloomy economic news?

Dr. Lopez: When workers think about ideas and energy for the future, they may have energy and a big goal, but they don't have specific ideas about how to get there. This kind of low hope — high energy and low ideas — is the easiest for managers to fix. When workers are thinking about a goal and then an obstacle pops up, their manager can get them unstuck by showing them how others [accomplished that goal], showing them new pathways, helping them think things through.

Really, there are lots of ways to get unstuck. The energy to achieve the goals — the force that moves them from point A to point B — is actually harder to inspire than the ideas. You can give employees more ideas, but to energize them to the point that they can start moving again, that takes deep, mentoring relationships. But sometimes a jolt of positive emotion can help them get unstuck. A new vision of the goal, something that makes it seem more attainable, can help them get unstuck. But it's hard to breathe new life into employees. It's easier for managers to marshal the strategic resources than to energize workers.

GMJ: But can managers actually instill hope? Can anyone do this? Or is hope innate?

Dr. Lopez: The wacky thing is we're the only creatures on the planet who really have a complex view of the future. What I struggle with is when people don't capitalize on this uniquely human quality.

A friend of mine has a Saint Bernard, and she has this little bitty sliding gate protecting the kitchen from the dog or the dog from the kitchen. And the gate barely works — it's just kind of rigged up. So I asked, "Can't the dog easily knock over this gate?" And my friend said, "Yeah, but he doesn't know he can. He just stands on the other side and waits for me to open it."

And that's the thing — managers need to know that they can take advantage of this horsepower humans have to set goals and move toward the future in a powerful way. When we experience uncertainty, which we're going through right now, we slow down. Fear puts blinders on us, and it keeps us in a smaller social space. So we don't reach out as much, and we don't socialize as much; all kinds of bad indicators go up, and all kinds of good indicators go down. When we're fearful, we shut down, and we don't think clearly about our options.

That's what's happening now, and hope is actually an antidote to all that. Hope is an antidote to fear. It gives us enough belief that good things can happen in the future that we can take the blinders off and expand our social circles. The bigger our social circles, the more resources we have. When we think about survival of the fittest, humans who have a lot of social capital actually do better than humans who have very low social capital. So if we're able to take the blinders off, see opportunities where other people see catastrophes, and make sure we maintain the social capital around us, then we're able to keep moving toward the goals that matter to us most.

GMJ: What about managers who have to fire people? What can they say to keep the people they must fire hopeful?

Dr. Lopez: Your responsibility in that situation is to be as honest and straightforward as possible. Respect the fear that the person is experiencing: "I know you're scared about your future and the future of those around you." That kicks off a psychological process in which they can manage the fear a little bit better and with a little more dignity as well.

But the reality is that losing a job can send folks into an abyss of uncertainty and give them an unfocused, damaged relationship with the future. When you have a damaged relationship with the future, that's when hopelessness can creep in. That's when bad things can happen on a personal level.

So a great way to go about helping people transition is to help them frame the future a little bit. Companies that can offer some kind of severance pay or job transition opportunity — coaching, career counseling, something like that — will help frame the future so that folks can remain hopeful. Retraining helps people reinvent that relationship with the future.

Sending people from the point of termination to the next place is vital. If you're interested in the welfare of the folks who are being laid off, you need to make sure they have enough pieces to start reframing their relationship with the future. And if they have those pieces, they can remain hopeful enough to keep moving in a healthy, safe, somewhat positive direction. If you throw them into an abyss and don't respect the fact that they're fearful and overwhelmed by uncertainty, then there's no real jump-start for them to start creating that new future.

Those are the folks I'm particularly concerned about because they're stuck. They don't have goals, they don't have the energy to move, and they don't have many ideas about the direction to move in. So whatever companies can do to help these employees make a meaningful transition will make a big difference on an individual level — and it can also make a big difference on a societal level.

GMJ: *A big part of being a company leader is putting on a "game face" — projecting hope, optimism, and a can-do spirit. What would you say to leaders who, in quiet moments and in the face of this relentless economic crisis, feel hopeless themselves?*

Dr. Lopez: Company leaders certainly have their dark moments, and they should share these struggles with their closest confidants. They should surround themselves with hopeful people who can get them unstuck.

Company leaders need to remember that their personal hope is a public resource. Employees look to leaders to capitalize on the spirit and ideas of the times, to dream big, and to motivate them toward a virtuous future. If you can't make your employees excited about the future, you're no longer a leader.

DISENGAGEMENT CAN BE REALLY DEPRESSING
by Jennifer Robison

April 2, 2010

Gallup has studied employee engagement for decades. Researchers have interviewed millions of people in numerous job roles in hundreds of companies all over the world. Over and over, Gallup has found that engagement — an emotional and psychological bond between workers and workplaces — leads to better work performance.

But recently, Gallup discovered that better employee engagement means better health too. "Engaged people feel less stress, and the stress they do feel is offset by a lot more happiness and enjoyment and interest," says Jim Harter, Ph.D., Gallup's chief scientist of workplace management and wellbeing and coauthor of *12: The Elements of Great Managing*.

The converse is true of the disengaged, who feel more stress and have fewer sources of pleasure at work. "There's a significant relationship between work, stress, and health," Harter says. "In other words, if people are in an ongoing work situation that is negative or stressful, they have a higher potential for negative health consequences."

Disengagement and mental health
Those health consequences have been associated with a variety of illnesses in people over the age of 45 — and not just ailments of age. The quality of the workplace can be linked to serious physical and mental illnesses such as clinical depression and chronic anxiety that can have a significant negative impact on workers' job performance and on their personal lives.

Anxiety and depression can be serious conditions that undermine daily functioning and health. According to the National Institute of Mental Health (NIMH), anxiety, typically a normal reaction to stress, becomes debilitating when it becomes "an excessive, irrational dread of everyday situations." In a given year, approximately 40 million U.S. adults (18 and older) — about 18% of the U.S. population — are affected by an anxiety disorder.

Depression, according to NIMH, interferes with daily life and normal functioning. While the symptoms of depression vary depending on the individual and his or her illness, they include "persistent sad, anxious or 'empty' feelings; feelings of hopelessness and/or pessimism; . . . loss of interest in activities or hobbies once pleasurable; . . . fatigue and decreased energy; [and] difficulty concentrating, remembering details and making decisions." About 14.8 million American adults, or about 7% of the U.S. population aged 18 and older, are affected by depression in a given year.

Not only do anxiety and depression take a personal toll on workers, but they also result in significant direct costs to businesses in medical expenses — and indirect costs, including lost productivity. In 2000, for example, the economic burden of depression in the United States was estimated at $83.1 billion, which included $26.1 billion in direct treatment costs and $51.5 billion in indirect workplace costs from absenteeism and "presenteeism," or reduced productivity while at work due to depression. And a 2003 study found that workers with depression reported an average of 5.6 hours of lost productive time at work each week, compared with an expected 1.5 hours of lost productive time among workers without depression.

A recent Gallup study into the effects of disengagement on mental health — conducted February 2008 through April 2009 — studied U.S. workers as the country moved through the recession. At the start of the study, which involved 9,561 employed adults, Gallup asked respondents whether they had ever been diagnosed by a healthcare professional as suffering from a variety of medical conditions, including depression and anxiety. Respondents with a previous diagnosis of depression or anxiety were excluded from the analysis. Respondents were also asked Gallup's 12-item employee engagement assessment, the Q^{12}, which determines an individual's level of engagement with his or her workplace.

When these respondents were surveyed again about eight months later, Gallup found that 6.4% of engaged workers had been diagnosed with anxiety, compared with 7.6% of not-engaged workers and 10.4% of actively disengaged workers. And 4.6% of engaged workers had been diagnosed with depression, as had 6% of not-engaged workers and 8.8% of actively disengaged workers. In other words, actively disengaged employees were 1.7 times as likely as engaged employees to report being diagnosed with anxiety for the first time in the next year. And actively disengaged employees were almost twice as likely as engaged employees to report being diagnosed with depression for the first time in the next year.

The connection between the quality of a workplace and employee engagement is well-established. What's more, engagement has proved to be a powerful predictor of many key organizational outcomes, including profitability, productivity, customer engagement, quality, safety, and retention. This research shows that there is a strong connection between engagement and important individual outcomes, such as employees' mental health.

References

Greenberg, P.E., Kessler, R.C., Birnbaum, H.G., Leong, S.A., Lowe, S.W., Berglund, P.A., et al. (2003). The economic burden of depression in the United States: How did it change between 1990 and 2000? *The Journal of Clinical Psychiatry, 64*(12), 1465-1475.

Stewart, W.F., Ricci, J.A., Chee, E., Hahn, S.R., Morganstein, D. (2003). Cost of lost productive work time among US workers with depression. *The Journal of the American Medical Association, 289*(23), 3135-3144.

OVERCOMING THE FEAR OF CHANGE

An interview with David Jones, change consultant
by Jennifer Robison

January 7, 2011

There are people who recoil from change no matter how necessary the change is. And there are others who love change for change's sake. The first type can prohibit progress; the second can cause chaos. And both probably exist in your organization. The problem is that you can't dismiss the fears of the first type or the adventurousness of the second. Either group might be right about change initiatives. A leader's job is to make the call, then guide both groups through the organization's transformation.

That's not easy, according to David Jones. For more than 20 years, Jones has consulted with some of America's biggest companies — including Ameritrade, Bon Secours Health System, and Blue Cross/Blue Shield — introducing and directing change. Assessing the potential of a change is one of the hardest, and most important, parts of a leader's job, says Jones.

But making the decision to change is only the first step in the change process. There are good ways and bad ways to alter an organization, lots of mistakes change agents can make, and pitfalls galore. In the following conversation, Jones explains why change initiatives usually fail, why it's better to take small steps than change everything at once, how to get people on board and keep them there, and what challenges to expect along the way.

Gallup Management Journal: *How do you know when a change is required?*

David Jones: First, identify why the organization is considering a change in the first place. Some people call that process strategic intent. But it's simply understanding where the change originates, what we want to accomplish with it, and why we would even do this. The truth is that people really don't like change. Change is hard, it's costly, it disrupts the norm, and it requires us to do things differently. Everything in us would rather stick with the status quo. That's why most changes in business are unsuccessful and don't meet the expectations laid out for them.

The most important issue is getting clear about why you need to make a change. Is there a business imperative? Will it deliver value that justifies the expense and disruption? That's important because when you get into the change process, you're going to find out it's harder than you thought, it will take longer than you thought, it'll probably cost more than you thought, and it will be more disruptive than you thought. You need to be clear up front about what you are doing, why you are doing it, how it will make your organization different, and why the change is really critical to your organization's success.

GMJ: Which is more effective: radical change or slow, small steps?

Jones: Change rarely succeeds; it's very costly, very difficult. But the changes that are most successful are changes that are consistent with the culture of the organization, that are incremental in nature, that don't push people too far out of their comfort zone, and that can be staged over a longer period of time. It's also good to test things — to do a pilot or get people on board gradually. I was at Bon Secours for 10 years, and even though they weren't ready for me at first, I had time to ease off and make things more palatable. We tested structural changes and new programs at some facilities, watched what worked, and then implemented what succeeded elsewhere.

My first experience was in a medium-sized community hospital, and I had two years to get to know the people and the culture and to test things out slowly and gradually before a new CEO came in and everything moved into the fast lane. But by then, I had credibility. We changed lots of things: pay systems, the performance management system, and many other human resources programs. But none of it seemed radical. It worked because I was known and trusted.

Incremental changes are the better way to go because they're more successful, people adapt to them more readily, and they're more sustainable. Take on transformational change only when you have to.

GMJ: How do you know when you have to?

Jones: Business dynamics, technology, competition, the economy, globalization, and such sometimes require us to make changes that are radical and transformational. When that's the case, we have to *know* that's the case, and the change has got to be tied to something critical for the organization's success.

Several years ago, I was brought into a small community hospital in West Virginia that was reacting to tremendous changes in the industry: HMOs were coming in, there were new competitors, and there were radical changes in the way the government paid for services. At that point, we simply couldn't do business the way we'd always done it — our old business model was now a "go-out-of-business" strategy. It required transformational change. So the CEO became the change sponsor. I was the change agent. And we marshaled the forces and organized a new model.

GMJ: How was it received?

Jones: At first, badly. A lot of people had been there their whole careers; many weren't reading the trade magazines or talking to people in other hospitals. They were unaware of the changed environment, and they liked the way they were working. Some people said we were trying to bring in Japanese management techniques. They thought I was some big-city guy telling them what to do. There was even a union organization drive in response.

It wasn't just the frontline workers who were unhappy, either, because almost everyone had to change in some way. Leadership had been leading by command and control and didn't know how to delegate. There were skill deficiencies, but the new working environment required a lot more self-sufficiency at all levels and more local decision making. We had to overcome a lot of obstacles. But that's the point — we had to change to survive. And eventually, we did.

GMJ: What's the difference between a change sponsor and a change agent?

Jones: If you're the person sponsoring the change, you have the ability to initiate the change, to provide the resources, and to hold people accountable. Sponsorship is when the leaders look around and say, "Guess what — we've got to acquire our second largest competitor to gain an advantage in the marketplace." Then they create a new business strategy, which means change on a much larger scale.

Typically, these leaders then go to someone and say, "Here's what we need to make happen; I need your help to execute this." That person is the change agent. [The change agent] is not convincing them to do this; they're the ones who have the urgency. They're looking to you, the change agent, to figure out how to change successfully, and they need your support to help structure the change initiative and get other people excited about it.

But there's got to be somebody in the organization who has the clout and who can provide the sponsorship necessary for the change. Sponsors hold people's feet to the fire and identify those folks who may have something to lose; who may not be excited about the change; who may have to change themselves; and who may undermine, resist, or try to derail the change. Sponsors help hold those people accountable.

GMJ: What does it take to make both roles work in a change initiative?

Jones: The trick for the change agent is to be really, really clear with the sponsor as to what the sponsor is willing to do to make the change successful. Sometimes the change agent is more committed to a change than the sponsor, and then the agent must try to compensate for the lack of sponsorship.

For example, maybe the CEO isn't as visible as he needs to be around an initiative, so as change agents, we have to get out there and carry the message. Maybe the sponsor isn't sending out the communication, so we create our own communication vehicles. Maybe the sponsor isn't holding people accountable, so we're out there trying to tell people why it's important.

When that happens, people look around and say, "Well, I see you talking about this change, but I don't hear the CEO talking about it. Why isn't he out here? Why aren't leaders telling their people this is important? Why are you the face of this, and why have they gone quiet?" If you can't get your sponsor actively engaged to provide the leadership necessary, you can't succeed only on the strength of your desire to make this thing happen.

GMJ: *Then what should you do?*

Jones: You've got to back up, slow down, and re-engage your sponsor. If the sponsor is unwilling or unable to play his required role, that is your signal that the change is no longer important. Without adequate sponsorship, the change initiative will eventually fail, and you, the agent, will be blamed.

To make change, you've got to constantly retest the sponsors' commitment and resolve. One of the things a good change agent does is discourage leaders from initiating change when it won't be sustained or when leaders don't really understand what they're getting themselves into. It's crucial to test sponsors' commitment repeatedly so that down the road they don't say, "This really is a lot more work than we thought. We really had no idea it would take this long or cost this much, and if we had known, we wouldn't have started it." When people backtrack, you lose so much time and energy — and you lose credibility and productivity.

GMJ: *Then change becomes much harder the next time.*

Jones: That's exactly right. Then you get what we call "change history" — your record of starting, sustaining, and finishing change. If you have a good change history — of doing the right things in moderation over time or making key strategic decisions and executing them effectively — then when it comes time for the next thing, people will be a lot more excited and motivated than if you're somebody who starts a lot of things without a lot of forethought and then abandons them.

I've been in a lot of organizations where employees think, "I'm going to wait this change initiative out. I've seen these come and go. I've seen leaders come and go. I've heard these words and phrases before. I'm not going to get excited about this, because I know it's not going to last." That's the worst situation you can be in: when you desperately need to make a major change and nobody believes you because you've cried wolf too many times.

It's much better to start fewer things and do them effectively, especially large-scale changes. People are busy, and they don't like disruption unless there's a good reason for it. Show them that change will make their lives better. Make the case that we're bringing an innovation, a solution, or a change that will solve a real-time problem or fix a pain point.

GMJ: Can you give me an example?

Jones: I saw this with a diversity program in a financial services company. At first, it seemed like a great idea, and we jumped on the bandwagon. But over time, enthusiasm waned, and it became clear that leaders, managers, and employees would have to make significant changes. It was going to take time to see results, and some of the issues that surfaced were ingrained in the culture and caused people a great deal of discomfort. It became easier to have a marginal program than to push the organization to make the meaningful and sustainable changes.

Our experience was not unique. Very few companies can make a commitment to sustain changes over time and make the difficult decisions and investments that change requires. Many programs are either marginalized or abandoned when the price of change becomes prohibitively high. When that happens, they fail to meet the original expectations.

GMJ: What are good metrics for assessing whether a change is successful?

Jones: First, define the strategic intent or the business imperative that you're trying to accomplish. Get very clear about how you will measure success. Then determine whether you can use the same metrics you already have in place that define your business success — growth, profitability, margins, employee engagement, balance sheet, productivity, the strength of your talent pool.

One of the reasons that change initiatives fail is that organizations don't spend the time up front deciding why they're doing this, what it will do for them, and how they'll measure success. One result is that they redefine success by lowering their expectations.

You can tell things are going badly if the change starts with fanfare but ends on a whimper. Nobody calls a meeting or puts a blog out or has a big celebration to announce you're not doing this anymore. People just stop talking about it. The more disciplined and specific you are up front, the clearer your implementation structure and metrics will be. It also will be easier to keep people's focus on how a change helps meet goals.

GMJ: Does change get easier then?

Jones: No, it gets harder. Once you get past the novelty of a change, you'll find that every system in your organization is set up to reject it. You've got to have the resolve, the courage, and the fortitude to see change through that part of the process, because it's the most difficult part of the transition. You'll only accomplish that if you're able to successfully communicate why you're changing, how it will be measured, why it is critical, and why people need to get on board and make this successful.

When I was working at a hospital in Nebraska, I was doing a reorganization in human resources while also driving a bigger organizational change agenda. Within three months, I started getting a lot of pushback. The change sponsor had a hotline for people to use with questions and concerns, and the sponsor's assistant called to tell me they were getting a lot of pushback, so I asked her to transcribe the comments.

I came in on a Saturday to read the stack from my own folks, and that was one of the worst days of my working life. There was so much fear, so much misunderstanding — even though we had meetings, sent newsletters, used every form of communication. I had to re-evaluate why we were doing this, whether it was an ego trip, whether it was worth doing. I had to go back to our original survey where employees talked again and again about what wasn't working and why they weren't engaged. But many of my staff weren't excited about the change, and the further we went, the more alienated they became.

So we did some team building, took more care of people emotionally, made sure people were involved and heard, and got out more data about what we were doing and why it was good for customers. It's easy to get out of touch with the emotions of the people most affected by change.

STRATEGIES FOR THE "NEW NORMAL"

PLANNING FOR THE "NEW NORMAL"
by William J. McEwen

June 9, 2009

Depending on who's reading the economic tea leaves, there are some signs that things may be getting better. Or maybe they've just stopped getting worse. The cautiously bullish "signs of stability" and "bottom has been reached" comments of some company CEOs may perhaps be tinged as much by wishful thinking as by hard data. Certainly, the supporting evidence is mixed. Nevertheless, companies are talking about the future and gearing up for the challenges they'll face once things settle down.

And they will settle down, won't they?

That depends on what we mean by "settle down." Many analysts are convinced that the post-recession environment will look nothing like the marketing world we once knew or thought we knew. Some forecasters are predicting a new world that will be populated with smaller, greener cars. Some anticipate a sharp decrease in home ownership, with smaller homes that have a lot less "stuff" in them. There's talk about a future where consumers will be far more conservative in their investments and where they'll be saving more and spending less.

Even the most optimistic company leaders acknowledge that a revival in consumer spending won't be happening in the next few fiscal quarters. Gallup's U.S. polls report that consumer spending remains flat, and more than half of consumers (58%, as of June 9) feel that the economy is still getting worse. In any case, whenever this hoped-for spending resurgence does begin to show itself, the expectation is that business will definitely not be "as usual."

Some business leaders anticipate that consumers will be much more demanding because they'll remain highly sensitive to price yet also intolerant of poor quality or poor service. So a strategy that involves cutting prices by skimping on performance isn't likely to thrill the customer or ensure loyalty. Many executives expect that today's altered patterns of shopping and buying will remain, that the current intense focus on value for money will endure, and that consumers will never return to their old habits. Some contend that there have been "profound shifts" in shoppers' psychology and that, at least for luxury retailers, "the party's over."

Lessons from the past

But forecasters must bear in mind that the consumers of tomorrow, just like the consumers of yesterday, have emotional needs that are as essential as their rational, functional needs — and prognosticators must take these emotional needs into account. When consumers were confronted with skyrocketing gas prices and long service station lines during the 1973 oil embargo, some analysts decreed that U.S. auto buyers would forever abandon the large gas-guzzling cars that had typified the U.S. market. The future, they contended, would be all about small fuel-efficient cars. U.S. manufacturers responded, downsizing their vehicles and equipping them with 4-cylinder engines. This, the thinking went, would be the "new normal" for the 1980s and beyond.

But U.S. auto buyers were never focused solely on obtaining better gas mileage, particularly if it came at the cost of vehicle reliability or safety. U.S. consumers wanted vehicles that did more than meet their functional needs (allowing them to get from point A to point B); they wanted cars that also met their emotional needs (the desire for a passionate personal connection to the vehicle they own). Buyers wanted better gas mileage, to be sure, but they also wanted sexy style, riding comfort, and driving performance. They still wanted to feel good about the car they were driving; they still wanted to feel proud. They did ask for fuel efficiency, but they didn't ask for boring.

So, the new small, soulless, gas-efficient boxes were soon replaced by sportier, peppier alternatives, often provided by imports. And in direct contrast with the expectations of some pundits, the route was being paved for the ultimate emergence of the Hummer, which is hardly the type of vehicle predicted by those who were watching the initial, rational, consumer response to an unprecedented marketplace shock.

The world today may well be sharply different from the one that existed four decades ago. Yet there are some evident caveats for anyone aiming to market to the consumers who will be emerging from the current unprecedented bubble-bursting economic slump: Never ignore the emotional component.

First, let's look at what's happening at the moment. McDonald's has been doing very well, selling its value meals while marketing its coffee in competition with higher priced Starbucks. Wal-Mart has shown real growth, and in the U.K., price-focused Morrisons has been outperforming its supermarket rivals. Grocery and convenience store shoppers have been turning to less expensive private-label goods, and consumers are increasingly clipping and redeeming coupons.

In response to price-sensitive shoppers, retailers have been diligently slashing their prices and demanding that companies that make the products they carry do likewise. Diners have been scaling back their taste for fancy foods and fancy restaurants, and shoppers appear to be shunning frills and emphasizing essentials. But are these changes merely short-term coping mechanisms, or are they the harbinger of totally new shopping patterns and habits?

A future without frills?

The critical question isn't so much what consumers are doing now but whether they'll keep doing it in the future. Of course, time will tell. But regardless of the accuracy of the "new normal" forecasts, many retailers are already actively preparing for what they believe will come next. Tesco is reportedly investing $225 million to relaunch its loyalty program. Grocers such as ALDI are building new distribution centers. Some of the big retail chains are expanding, with Dollar General and CVS joining Walgreens and Wal-Mart in planning to add hundreds of new stores to extend their reach.

Despite the seeming power of a price promise, successful long-term marketing will never be just about meeting consumers' functional needs. Consumer-perceived brand value involves a whole lot more than just price.

In truth, much of what's "new" about all this is actually not all that new. In working with marketers in categories ranging from supermarkets and banks to hotels and autos, Gallup has learned that there are fundamental prerequisites for a healthy brand, whether times are good or bad. Healthy brands are those that develop and nurture engaged customer relationships.

The essential bedrock for an enduring relationship has always been, and will always be, customer confidence. And that foundation, for many companies and in many industries, has been shaken. Marketing organizations that are surviving — and thriving — will be those that address the need to rebuild this foundation with meaningful promises that can and will be kept at every customer encounter. Price is only one promise, and long term, it may not speak to the consumers' emotional needs or their desire for self-expression.

Consumers will remain cautious about what they buy and when they buy it. But the "new normal" isn't likely to be a world where consumers continually deny themselves the personal rewards — small or large — that they feel they've earned. Yet they'll be choosy, perhaps more so than ever before. They know they have options. Thanks in part to the Internet, they now have the means to learn a whole lot about these options, often by hearing the voices of other customers — the engaged as well as the disengaged. (See "How Engaged Are Your Customers?" in the Appendix.)

The "new normal" probably will reveal a generally more skeptical consumer, one who feels burned by too many overstated or broken promises. This consumer may be more wary and less readily accepting of company reports, claims, and statements of intent. So, for at least the next few quarters, consumers in many parts of the world are going to be a lot like meerkats. They'll be guardedly poking their heads up to see where the dangers may lie.

Since trust has been dramatically called into question, tomorrow's meerkat consumers will be on the lookout for products and services — and companies — that they can believe in and that are demonstrably worthy of their patronage. They may be more willing to switch and to try new solutions. It's certainly possible that they'll abandon their old habits and old brands, but they'll do so for the very same reasons they always have: promises that fail to truly resonate; promises that are made but not kept.

In the "new normal," a few things seem clear. The consumer is now in charge. And the consumer will continue to have emotional needs as well as functional requirements. The companies that recognize this and act accordingly will be the ones that will prosper. It's a daunting challenge, to be sure, but it's also a singular opportunity.

A POWERFUL ALTERNATIVE TO CUTTING COSTS

by John H. Fleming

October 6, 2009

2009 has been a tough year for economies around the world as credit markets and consumer spending remain constrained. The latest Gallup consumer research shows that consumer confidence in the United States is improving somewhat, but spending levels in 2009 remain well below those in 2008. According to the U.S. Department of Commerce, retail sales in the United States through July of 2009 (excluding automobiles) were down approximately 9% compared to the same period last year. None of this is good news.

Against this bleak backdrop, retailers and other companies around the world are struggling to find ways to do more with less — and to keep moving forward against serious headwinds. Many retailers continue to trim budgets, lay off employees, and even close locations. While many of these steps seem like obvious and even responsible responses to the current economic environment, Gallup research suggests that there are other, perhaps less obvious, steps that companies can take to successfully navigate this sluggish economy and to buy time and remain financially viable until conditions improve. But instead of relying solely on cost curtailment, downsizing, and organizational realignments, these steps focus on optimizing the human element of your business by engaging your staff and your customers.

For more than 10 years, Gallup research has consistently found that engaged workgroups are more productive and profitable — and deliver superior customer outcomes — compared to their disengaged counterparts. Engaged workgroups have significantly better staff retention, lower absenteeism, fewer accidents, and yield lower levels of "shrink" (e.g., theft or breakage) than disengaged workgroups. These kinds of cost reductions not only result in greater operating efficiencies, but those benefits accrue to your bottom line as well.

Gallup research also has consistently found that emotionally engaged customers deliver superior financial returns than disengaged customers. Fully engaged customers deliver a 23% premium in terms of share of wallet, profitability, revenue, and relationship growth than the average customer, while disengaged customers deliver a 13% *discount*. Moreover, local work units that engage customers at high levels deliver significantly better financial performance (on the order of two times better) than low-engagement units.

Our research, which is described in detail in the book *Human Sigma: Managing the Employee-Customer Encounter* (Gallup Press, 2007), suggests that optimizing both of these human elements delivers significantly stronger financial performance than focusing on either in isolation. In fact, units in your organization that simultaneously optimize both employee and customer engagement significantly outperform units that optimize just employee or customer engagement — or fail to optimize either element — on measures of financial and operational success.

Much of our analysis of the financial impact of HumanSigma management — managing both employee and customer engagement in tandem, rather than independently — has been conducted during reasonably "normal" economic circumstances. But what about in conditions like those that prevail today? How well can managing your company's employee and customer engagement help when markets are turbulent and trending down? Fortunately, some recent data in the retail and retail banking industries can help answer this question.

HumanSigma management at a large retailer
Retailer H is a large multisite, multiformat retailer located in North America. It operates more than 400 stores and has been working on its HumanSigma performance for the past two years. Over the past year, the company has seen dramatic improvement in its HumanSigma performance. One year ago, just 3% of its stores were "optimized" — that is, just 3% of its stores had both employee and customer engagement scores above the 50th percentile in Gallup's retail database. However, after just one year of active intervention at the store level, almost half (47%)

of its stores had improved by at least one HumanSigma level, pushing an additional 18% of stores into the optimized performance band.

How did Retailer H accomplish this? Gallup has found that one of the surest ways to drive organizational change is to focus action locally — where employees spend the bulk of their time and where customer interactions happen. In our experience, teams that share and discuss their results, develop realistic and specific action plans, and then follow through on those plans almost invariably improve.

The active interventions at Retailer H included a range of activities at the local, team, and enterprise levels. Chief among these was local action planning related to local teams' and stores' employee and customer engagement scores; these plans were designed to address the unique issues affecting local teams and stores. These action-planning activities were intentionally kept simple. Each store team focused on just one or two improvement opportunities.

None of these local actions, however, would have been possible without the active support of the leadership and headquarters teams. Supporting these local activities at the enterprise level allowed Retailer H to build an infrastructure to facilitate its "think globally, act locally" focus.

In addition to the actions taken at the store and team level, Retailer H identified and deployed a team of internal champions who acted as local engagement coaches for the store teams. Leadership coaching of mid-level and senior-level executives provided leaders with opportunities to understand their individual performance results. The coaches also helped leaders think about their own levels of engagement and brainstorm ways that they could involve their teams in creating solutions.

Focused and uniquely branded program launch events helped to create a foundation of understanding across the enterprise. They also provided a means for all staff to apply the tools to their stores in an individualized way.

For any large organization, such substantial performance shifts represent exceptional levels of improvement. But the most impressive aspect of Retailer H's performance was that this was all done against a backdrop of declining retail sales across North America.

Equally impressive, however, were the financial results that followed. During the time Retailer H was undertaking these efforts, same-store sales (year over year) for the chain as a whole declined by 1.3%, and profit declined by more than 3%. But in the highest performing stores — those that were optimized — sales and profit actually *grew* by approximately 1% and 0.4%, respectively. In contrast, in the poorest performing stores in HumanSigma levels 1 or 2, sales and profit *declined* by roughly two times the company average.

Against the overall company's declining sales and profit performance, stores that improved their HumanSigma performance held their own in same-store sales (losing just 0.1%) and had profit declines that were about one-third smaller than the company average.

HumanSigma at a community bank

Retail Bank W is a community bank with more than $3 billion in assets and more than 30 branches. The bank has been working on improving its HumanSigma performance for the past five years. Like Retailer H, over the past year, the company has also seen dramatic improvement in its HumanSigma performance.

One year ago, a respectable 75% of its branches were optimized. Less than 5% of its branches were in HumanSigma levels 1 or 2 (the two lowest performing bands), but the momentum had stalled. However, after a year of reinvigorated intervention at the enterprise and branch levels, almost half (41%) of its branches had improved by at least one HumanSigma level, pushing an additional 16% into the optimized quadrant (and most of those moving into level 6, the highest performance band).

Like Retailer H, these interventions included a range of activities at both the local and the enterprise levels. Chief among the activities at the local level was a renewed focus on local action planning on the bank's employee and customer engagement scores, a focus that had been lost during the time momentum had stalled.

Retail Bank W also took action at the enterprise level. In addition to making a number of leadership changes, Bank W's CEO recommitted to his role as a true engagement champion. Employee and customer engagement are always on his agenda: Engagement is a continual topic of conversation in meetings, e-mails, and addresses to the company. As he makes his rounds throughout the company, he personally comments on the success stories that circulate within the company, and he congratulates the successful teams.

As proof of his commitment to driving higher levels of performance, the CEO also challenged his organization to meet the goal of "90/90" — to be at the 90th percentile on both employee and customer engagement. He's made this an inspirational goal, though, rather than a punitive target. Bank W's leadership does not hound business units to reach an arbitrary number, which could lead to undesired behaviors. Instead, the CEO uses the target to paint a vision of the future for his organization. Our consultants speak to a lot of executive leadership teams about the importance of executive buy-in, support, and modeling behavior as a means to create an environment where engagement can flourish. They never have to have that conversation at Bank W.

Beyond personally "walking the talk," Bank W's CEO also created a new position: HumanSigma manager. This manager, who reports directly to him, is responsible for coordinating and aligning all employee and customer engagement activities. The HumanSigma manager works on an individual level with many of the bank's teams, especially those that have continually struggled to improve their engagement performance. She is in the branches every week, making sure that managers and teams have enough support to perform effective impact planning.

Finally, in an effort to facilitate the bank's continued momentum and growth, the HumanSigma manager has begun to help the bank focus on the individual strengths of its employees. She and other staff members are certified as Strengths Performance Coaches, and they coach managers one-on-one to support them in using their strengths to boost individual and team performance. Bank W also sends its managers through the Gallup Great Manager Program, a program designed to help their best managers become even better — faster.

These kinds of performance improvements are impressive under optimal conditions, but they are even more impressive considering that they were all accomplished against the well-publicized difficulties in the retail banking sector. More importantly, this concerted focus on improving employee and customer engagement has paid off handsomely for Bank W. While other retail banks have announced layoffs and other cost-cutting measures, Bank W has remained steady and on course. Compared to its industry peers, whose earnings per share (EPS) dropped by an average of 33% during 2008, Bank W's EPS dropped by less than a third of that (9%).

And for the preceding year, which could best be described as a mixed economic environment, Bank W's EPS performance actually improved by 4% while its peer group's EPS declined by 8%. Even during the good economic environment from 2004 to 2007, focusing on engagement paid off for Bank W. During that period, its earnings continued to outpace those of its peers, growing 12% compared to a net decline of 2% among those peers.

These two case studies dramatically illustrate the impact that managing your company's HumanSigma performance can have on the top and bottom lines, even — and perhaps especially — in times of economic uncertainty and downturn. Gallup has estimated that the improvements at Retailer H conservatively netted $16 million in additional sales and about $8 million in additional margin on an annualized basis.

So rather than looking just to cost-saving measures to shore up your financials, look also to optimizing your HumanSigma. Not only will your organization be more likely to hold its own, but it will be ideally positioned for success when conditions improve.

ENGAGING PATIENTS IN A GLOBAL MARKET

by Maggie Ozan-Rafferty

December 17, 2009

Until fairly recently, the world looked to the West for the highest quality healthcare. Medicine in developing countries was not as advanced or as readily available as that found in Western countries. So those who wanted the best care — and who could afford it — booked flights to Europe or the United States.

But they don't have to anymore. As healthcare improves worldwide, consumers in many countries can be treated by local healthcare providers and receive care that is as good as or better than the care they'd receive in the West. Or they can choose to travel the world for the best quality healthcare at the best price. That's because world-class healthcare is becoming readily available internationally — and often for very affordable rates.

This has not escaped the notice of healthcare consumers. The trend is so pronounced that it has a moniker — medical tourism — and a growing share of the world's healthcare dollars and euros. In America alone, an estimated 750,000 people went overseas for medical treatment in 2007, and an estimated 1.6 million could travel for their healthcare by 2012, according to a 2009 study by the Deloitte Center for Health Solutions. And Gallup research shows that 29% of Americans would consider traveling to another country for a variety of medical procedures, including heart bypass surgery, hip or knee replacement, plastic surgery, cancer diagnosis and treatment, or alternative medical treatments.

Traveling internationally with a debilitating medical condition can be difficult, but it may save money. For example, a heart bypass surgery that runs $54,000 USD or more in the United States costs less than $10,000

USD in India. A hip replacement in the United States costs, on average, $45,000 USD; in Turkey, it can be had for $10,750 USD. And many patients who travel internationally for treatment are receiving excellent care. Among hospitals accredited by the Joint Commission International (JCI), a division of the Joint Commission, medical attention meets or exceeds the international standard.

As the world market for healthcare develops, medical tourism has rattled healthcare providers. For one thing, there are genuine concerns about long-distance travel for medical treatment. Continent hopping is arduous even for the most hardy; for the very ill, it can be perilous. Consumers also need to be wary that their hospital meets certain standards — facilities aren't required to be JCI accredited, after all. And even when the hospital provides excellent care and the treatment is flawless, after-care can be difficult to coordinate.

Those aren't the only concerns — there's also the impact that medical tourism can have on a hospital's bottom line. A 2008 study by the Deloitte Center for Health Solutions, for example, projected what Americans would spend on medical tourism. The study estimated that in 2008, Americans would spend $2.1 billion to obtain healthcare outside the United States, which represents an opportunity cost of $15.9 billion for U.S. healthcare providers. Given that the number of outbound American medical tourists could reach 1.6 million by 2012, this could translate into a loss of billions of dollars in revenue for U.S. providers, according to the Deloitte study.

Significant barriers

With an excellent standard of healthcare combined with low prices, it's a wonder medical tourism isn't more common. In fact, more people probably would travel for their medical care if it weren't for several significant barriers:

- Patients who require serious healthcare need reliable medical information, and it's not always easy to obtain such intelligence on hospitals outside one's home country.

- In the United States, most insurance companies don't cover non-urgent medical care in other countries. So it doesn't make economic sense to travel for treatment.

- Traveling internationally for surgery can be intimidating to coordinate. Many people don't want to face the difficulties of traveling to another country on top of the exigencies of recovering from surgery.

But given the widening market for healthcare, a number of businesses are helping consumers overcome these obstacles. Medical tourism is such a burgeoning industry that it has spawned subsidiary businesses that get, qualify, and publish data on the best hospitals worldwide. There are even travel agencies that do considerable legwork for patients, including providing information on hospitals, arranging travel and immediate post-care treatment, and coordinating after-care between patients' primary care physicians and the hospital abroad. So finding quality medical care, as well as getting after-care overseas or at home, is becoming less of a problem for consumers.

Increasingly, U.S. insurance companies are considering covering medical tourism, and some already do: BlueCross BlueShield of South Carolina, for instance, is stirring up the industry by adding several hospitals located outside the United States to its network and providing access to concierge services related to treatment. OptiMed Health/United Group has covered foreign medical care for more than a year, forgoing deductibles and co-pays and covering all travel expenses. Swiss Re's Commercial Insurance now recognizes medical travel coverage as part of its existing stop loss offering, which is offered through Westport Insurance Corp.

Some members of the business community aren't waiting for insurance companies to get around to covering healthcare overseas for their employees. Many companies, big and small, encourage (and pay for) medical tourism because it costs them so much less. Some have an informal, case-by-case policy offered more or less quietly. Others, such as the Hannaford Bros. Company, a grocery store chain based in Scarborough, Maine, are quite public, offering employees the option of getting hip and knee replacements in Singapore.

Engagement

So as quality healthcare becomes a global commodity — and as patients and companies contemplate the benefits of traveling abroad for the most cost-effective care — what can healthcare providers do to ensure that their patients are engaged and will return for service in the future? They can promote deep emotional bonds with their customers. This will make patients want to return for care — and encourage their friends and family to do so too.

It goes without saying that patients can develop deep emotional bonds with the people who heal them. If they do, patients can become fully engaged with their healthcare provider and/or the hospital. (See "How Engaged Are Your Customers?" in the Appendix.)

However, far too many healthcare facilities, regardless of where they're located, don't consider engagement when they think of their patient relationships. What most concern themselves with is patient satisfaction. U.S. hospitals in particular are well aware of their level of patient satisfaction. They have to be: The U.S. government mandates that hospitals survey patients about their satisfaction.

But satisfaction by itself isn't a good predictor of future customer behavior, as Gallup research has shown. Results from many case studies suggest that customers who provide the highest rating of overall satisfaction with a company's products or services — or those who are *extremely satisfied* — fall into two distinct groups:

- **Rationally satisfied** customers are extremely satisfied with the company but lack the strong emotional connection of customers who are emotionally satisfied.

- **Emotionally satisfied** customers are extremely satisfied with the products and services the company provides and have a strong emotional attachment to the company.

Emotionally satisfied customers deliver enhanced value to an organization by buying more, spending more, or returning more often to or staying longer with an organization. But rationally satisfied customers behave no differently than dissatisfied ones.

What *does* predict behavior is engagement, the profound psychological attachment customers develop for certain healthcare providers and medical centers — and patients *are* customers. And what patient engagement predicts is exactly the sort of thing all healthcare providers care about: fully engaged customers who are passionate about their providers and who are much likelier to return, to visit more often, to spend more per visit, and to make recommendations to their friends.

In a global healthcare market, you shouldn't take your fully engaged patients for granted; you must continually look for ways to build and maintain engaged relationships. For example, 54% of U.S. patients are fully engaged — and are far more likely to return for treatment to their American healthcare providers. But a $90,000 cost savings might be enough to make even a fully engaged patient think about traveling for more cost-effective treatment options — and less-engaged patients could be researching their options for medical care on the Internet right now.

As the playing field for quality healthcare goes global, simply competing on quality or price is not enough. The hospitals that will thrive in this new global marketplace — whether they are in North America, South America, Asia, Europe, or the Middle East — will be the ones that go beyond merely satisfying patients to fully engaging them.

RETAIL AND THE "NEW NORMAL"

by Ed O'Boyle, Rob Kroenert, Jessica Tyler, and Emily Meyer

April 27, 2010

Retail has always been a tough business. In the current economy, it's as tough as it's ever been. Gallup analysis suggests that there's a "new normal" for consumer spending — a fundamental shift in the way people spend and save. Even in an improving economy, we may discover that many consumers have permanently altered their shopping habits. Securing a share of a consumer's wallet may not get easier any time soon.

What does this mean for retailers? What is the secret to thriving in such a competitive environment?

For more than 40 years, Gallup has partnered with many of the world's top retailers. We have studied their brands, their customers, and their employees. Throughout the course of our work, one finding holds true: Stores that have a strong manager outperform other stores. The impact store managers have can't be overstated. They set the tone for the entire store and dramatically influence key performance metrics.

This won't surprise many retailers. What *is* surprising, however, is how frequently retailers fail to use this knowledge to their advantage. Too often, retailers pay lip service to the importance of store managers without creating the structure that's required to increase the impact of this crucial position.

Getting the most out of store managers

So how does a retailer create that necessary structure? Gallup has found that retailers can increase their store managers' performance by taking five key steps:

1. *Define the store manager's role.* Clearly identify the store manager's responsibilities and priorities.

2. *Find the right talent.* Match the store manager role with people who have the right talent to perform the role at excellence.

3. *Unleash your best.* Assign your best store managers to your best stores.

4. *Maximize strengths.* Invest in developing your store managers' strengths.

5. *Optimize local performance.* Provide your store managers with a system for managing the engagement of the associates in their stores.

Improvements in one area will support and enhance improvements in others, and progress on any one of these steps can make a difference. But addressing all the steps leads to the most dramatic progress. Let's look more closely at these five steps.

Step 1: Define the store manager's role

Store managers typically have an overwhelming range of responsibilities. They are under tremendous pressure to increase sales, minimize payroll, engage customers, control inventory, monitor shrinkage, forecast growth, hire and train employees — the list goes on and on.

Managers who are pulled in so many different directions will find it difficult to be effective if they aren't masters at prioritizing their time. Retailers can help their managers by determining which responsibilities they want them to focus on, then clearly defining the role to reflect those priorities.

One head of store operations at a leading retailer faced this challenge during his first week on the job. As part of his introductory tour, he asked store managers what prevented them from working with customers. The store managers said they were so busy filling out reports and complying with procedures that very little time remained for customers. The new head of store operations didn't like the sound of that. So he told the store managers to stop completing any reports that didn't help grow the business, and only start completing them again if someone complained.

It seems that most of the reports weren't missed, and the store managers gained an extra two hours each day to work with customers.

Removing the organizational barriers that block managers from increasing performance is crucial to success. But it's not easy to set these priorities; it requires difficult trade-offs. The best approach is to study how top-performing store managers allocate their time. This means retailers must be able to rank their store managers according to a defined set of performance criteria. That ranking can then be used to investigate the differences between the top performers and the lower performers and to draw lessons from those differences.

Once a retailer knows how it wants store managers to allocate their time, the next step is to incorporate those priorities into the formal job description and communicate the new expectations throughout the organization.

Step 2: Find the right talent

Something interesting happens when retailers define the role they want their store managers to play. They often discover that some of their current store managers aren't capable of being effective in that role.

The missing element is talent. Do your store managers have talent profiles that position them to excel in their role? In other words, do they have the recurring patterns of thought, feeling, and behavior that make them a match for the demands of the store manager position?

When reviewing the talents of their store managers, most retailers will find some whose talents are a poor fit to the role and who may need to be replaced. Selecting those replacements must be done with care to ensure that the new store managers have the right talent profile to succeed.

Gallup uses a scientific approach to this selection process. First, we identify the top performers in the role (this step may have already been completed during the definition of the store manager's role). Next, the top performers are compared and contrasted to a group of lower performing store managers. Gallup's research team looks for areas in which the top performers consistently think and behave differently than the lower performers. Those key areas become the basis of a selection instrument that can screen for candidates who match the talent profiles of the top-performing store managers.

This process works. Gallup finds that candidates with high scores on our selection instruments are much more likely to perform at a high level in the role. Over time, the instrument becomes even more accurate. We refine it by conducting validation studies that track the performance of high-scoring candidates to ensure that the right talent profiles are being selected.

Selecting the Right Manager Can Boost Store Performance

One of the best ways to increase retail store performance is to select the right store manager. Candidates with high scores on a scientifically designed selection instrument are much more likely to perform at a high level in the role. As this graph shows, annual profit at stores with managers who have a high talent score is significantly higher than at stores with lower scoring managers.

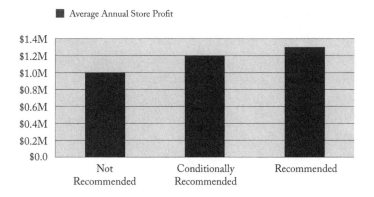

■ Average Annual Store Profit

Step 3: Unleash your best

Almost every retailer has "good" stores and "bad" stores. Good stores have few problems, are in prime locations, and make the most money. Bad stores experience one crisis after another, are in difficult locations, and struggle to make a profit. Dealing with bad stores is a constant challenge. One of the most common ways to deal with a bad store is to assign it to one of the company's best store managers, trusting the manager to turn things around. That makes sense, right?

Wrong. This is the *exact opposite* of what retailers should be doing. Instead, retailers should assign their *best* store managers to their *best* stores. The reason is simple: You get more bang for your buck. The impact a top-performing store manager can have on a good store far exceeds the impact he or she can have on a bad store.

In our work with a major electronics retailer, Gallup learned that strong store managers who engage employees and customers significantly improve their sales and profits whether they are in a good location or a bad one. However, great store managers can make dramatic improvements in stores that are already doing well; they usually make only modest improvements in stores that are mired in problems. In fact, we discovered that a larger chunk of missing growth was in locations that were deemed good. The bad ones already knew they had to turn over every possible rock to find growth opportunities. Gallup's extensive studies of employee performance have revealed this pattern repeatedly.

Step 4: Maximize strengths

For retailers to succeed, it's vital to have the right talents in the right roles. But it's just as important to invest in developing that talent. Most retailers provide their store managers with some kind of skills and competency training, but they stop there. That type of training, while necessary, isn't enough to drive real growth. Retailers that also identify and develop their store managers' strengths can significantly enhance their performance.

While a talent is a natural way of thinking, feeling, or behaving, developing a strength — the ability to consistently perform an activity at a near-perfect level — takes practice and hard work. But the effort yields a big payoff. Gallup's research has proven that helping employees leverage their strengths provides a range of benefits that far outweigh the investment.

Our studies show that a strengths-development program can increase a company's profitability, improve employee productivity, increase employee retention, and enhance customer engagement.

Step 5: Optimize local performance

A retailer that has taken the first four steps has now defined the store manager role, staffed the position with the right people, deployed them effectively, and invested in developing their strengths. This has created a formidable workforce that lacks just one thing: a structured system for measuring and managing employee and customer engagement.

Gallup's study of engagement is grounded in the emerging science of behavioral economics, led by notable scientists such as Princeton psychologist Daniel Kahneman, who won the Nobel Prize in economics. In contrast to traditional economic approaches, which assume that people are rational decision makers, behavioral economists theorize that rational considerations play a significantly smaller role than emotional factors in framing human decisions and behaviors. Behavioral economists theorize that only 30% of human decisions and behaviors are driven by rational considerations, meaning that more than two-thirds of the decisions that employees and customers make are based on emotional factors.

When someone is engaged, a meaningful connection has been established. Engaged employees are involved in and enthusiastic about their work and about contributing to their company's purpose and outcomes. Engaged customers are tied to a company by a meaningful bond that is both rational and emotional.

The connection between engagement and key business outcomes is measurable and powerful. Gallup research has found that in comparison to workgroups with disengaged employees, engaged workgroups are 18% more productive, 16% more profitable, 12% better at engaging customers, 37% less prone to absenteeism, and 27% less likely to be a source of inventory shrinkage.

Our studies have revealed similar connections between customer engagement and financial performance: Customers who are fully engaged represent an average 23% premium in terms of share of wallet, profitability, revenue, and relationship growth over the average customer. In stark contrast, actively disengaged customers represent a 13% *discount* in those same measures.

And optimizing both employee and customer engagement delivers significantly stronger financial performance than focusing on either in isolation. Workgroups that simultaneously optimize both elements significantly outperform workgroups that optimize just employee engagement or just customer engagement — or that fail to optimize either element — on measures of financial and operational success.

Implementing a system that enables store managers to optimize both employee and customer engagement provides them with the final piece of the puzzle they need to drive superior store performance. It gives managers the data they need to understand the engagement levels of their employees and their customers and provides them with a structured process for improving those engagement levels. Companies that have optimized their performance-management systems have outperformed their competitors by 26% in gross margin and 85% in sales growth. Their customers spend more, return more often, and stay longer.

Let's look at an example of how optimization works in the real world — and how it can help retailers achieve organic growth — in good and bad economic times. For the past two years, Gallup has worked with a large multisite, multiformat retailer on optimizing its customer and employee engagement. This retailer operates more than 400 stores in North America.

While this retailer was carrying out these efforts, same-store sales (year over year) for the chain as a whole declined by 1.3%, and profit declined by more than 3%. But in the highest performing stores — those that were optimized — sales and profit actually *grew* by approximately 1% and 0.4%, respectively. In contrast, in the poorest performing stores, sales and profit *declined* by roughly two times the company average.

Bucking the tide

The five steps outlined here — based on decades of Gallup research and analysis — represent the best strategy retailers can use to drive organic growth. Retailers that are seeking the single biggest leverage point in their company need look no further than their store managers. Taking effective action in any of the areas is a step in the right direction, but maximizing the performance of store managers by addressing all five of these areas will generate the biggest gains.

The old saying that "a rising tide lifts all boats" is only partially true. Even in a down economy, some retailers buck the tide and rise higher than the rest. The arrival of a "new normal" in consumer spending will make the market more competitive. To survive in a world where consumers are spending less and saving more, retailers need every edge they can get.

The Five Dimensions of Talent

Many organizations rely on experience, education, and skills or competencies when hiring for roles at all levels, and retailers are no exception. These qualifications alone, however, don't typically predict excellence in the role. Assessing whether an applicant has the talent to excel in the role is far more predictive of success, Gallup research indicates. And the degree of talent fit can best be determined by examining these five areas:

Motivation

How strong is your store managers' motivation? Do they bring energy and drive to what must be accomplished every day? What drives them to win? What numbers do they look at to determine if they are winning? Their enthusiasm, competitiveness, and need to achieve propels them to higher levels of productivity, service, and ultimately, repeat business.

Influence

Do your store managers consistently overcome obstacles? Are they able to inspire others to excel? Can they get their teams moving in the same direction and more consistently rally their associates to produce good results? The best store managers are visible, frequently in their store's aisles, and demonstrate the kind of customer interaction they want to see from their team members.

Workstyle

Do your managers demonstrate the ability to set goals, devise fun activities to reach those goals, and make sure that the important tasks are completed each day? Top-performing store managers inject a sense of urgency, and they love the fast-paced, ever-changing world that is retail. They sort to what is relevant and tend to see that customer-related and revenue-producing activities are among their most important daily priorities.

Relationship

Do your managers value people — customers *and* employees? The best managers see their business as centered on relationships. While part-time retail jobs are often temporary, many store managers started out in that role. They want the job to be fun, and they want their store associates to enjoy what they are doing: interacting with the customers, getting to know them and their needs, and helping them make purchases that meet those needs.

Thought Process

Do your store managers frequently think about the business as a business? Are they seeking ways to be creative and drive results? Are they smart about where their sales come from? Do they think about coverage and always make sure the store is adequately staffed during the busiest times? The best store managers are always thinking about how to improve results with the right ideas — and the right people driving performance.

APPENDIX

The Three Types of Employees

Gallup's employee engagement work is based on more than 30 years of research involving more than 17 million employees. Through this research, Gallup has defined three types of employees: engaged, not engaged, and actively disengaged.

- **Engaged** employees work with passion and feel a profound connection to their company. They drive innovation and move the organization forward.

- **Not engaged** employees are essentially "checked out." They're sleepwalking through their workday, putting time — but not energy or passion — into their work.

- **Actively disengaged** employees aren't just unhappy at work; they're busy acting out their unhappiness. Every day, these workers undermine what their engaged coworkers accomplish.

The 12 Elements of Great Managing

To identify the elements of worker engagement, Gallup conducted many thousands of interviews in all kinds of organizations, at all levels, in most industries, and in many countries. These 12 statements — the Gallup Q[12] — emerged from Gallup's pioneering research as those that best predict employee and workgroup performance. These 12 core elements link to key business outcomes, including earnings per share, profitability, safety incidents, and absenteeism.

1. I know what is expected of me at work.

2. I have the materials and equipment I need to do my work right.

3. At work, I have the opportunity to do what I do best every day.

4. In the last seven days, I have received recognition or praise for doing good work.

5. My supervisor, or someone at work, seems to care about me as a person.

6. There is someone at work who encourages my development.

7. At work, my opinions seem to count.

8. The mission or purpose of my company makes me feel my job is important.

9. My associates or fellow employees are committed to doing quality work.

10. I have a best friend at work.

11. In the last six months, someone at work has talked to me about my progress.

12. This last year, I have had opportunities at work to learn and grow.

How Engaged Are Your Customers?

Fully engaged customers are strongly emotionally attached and attitudinally loyal. They'll go out of their way to locate a favored product or service, and they won't accept substitutes. True brand ambassadors, they are your most valuable and profitable customers.

Engaged customers are emotionally attached, but they're not strongly loyal. They do like your product or service, but they can be tempted to switch by a more convenient, more attractive, or lower priced offer.

Not engaged customers have a "take it or leave it" attitude toward your product or service. They're disconnected emotionally and are attitudinally neutral toward your brand and what you're selling.

Actively disengaged customers are completely detached from your company and its products and services. They will readily switch or — if switching is difficult or impossible — may become virulently antagonistic toward your company or brand. Either way, they're always eager to tell others exactly how they feel.

CONTRIBUTING AUTHORS

Jim Clifton is the Chairman and CEO of Gallup.

Steve Crabtree is a writer for Gallup. He contributed to writing *Building Engaged Schools*, Gallup's book on education reform.

John H. Fleming, Ph.D., is Research Director and Chief Scientist — Customer Engagement and HumanSigma for Gallup. He is coauthor of *Human Sigma: Managing the Employee-Customer Encounter*.

Jim Harter, Ph.D., is Chief Scientist, Workplace Management and Wellbeing for Gallup's workplace management practice. He is coauthor of the *New York Times* bestsellers *12: The Elements of Great Managing* and *Wellbeing: The Five Essential Elements*.

Emily Killham is a former senior consultant for Gallup.

Rob Kroenert is former Practice Manager, Marketplace, for Gallup.

Jerry Krueger is a writer for Gallup.

William J. McEwen, Ph.D., is the author of *Married to the Brand* and coauthor of the *Harvard Business Review* article "Inside the Mind of the Chinese Consumer."

Emily Meyer is Practice Manager, Strengths-Based Selection and Development, for Gallup.

Ed O'Boyle is Practice Leader, Marketplace, for Gallup.

Bryant Ott is a writer and editor for Gallup.

Maggie Ozan-Rafferty is former Global Practice Leader, Healthcare, for Gallup.

Jennifer Robison is a Senior Editor of the *Gallup Management Journal*.

Benson Smith is coauthor of *Discover Your Sales Strengths*.

Jessica Tyler is Practice Leader, Employee Engagement and Wellbeing, for Gallup.

Rodd Wagner is a Senior Practice Consultant for Gallup. He is coauthor of the *New York Times* bestseller *12: The Elements of Great Managing* and *Power of 2: How to Make the Most of Your Partnerships at Work and in Life*.

Mick Zangari is a former senior consultant for Gallup.

ACKNOWLEDGEMENTS

We'd like to thank the following people for their outstanding work on this book and for their ongoing contributions to the *Gallup Management Journal:*

Kelly Henry, our peerless copyeditor.

Brandi Corbin, Bryant Ott, Julie Ray, Mark Stiemann, Alyssa Yell: superb editors who routinely offer their talents and expertise.

Kelly Slater, our inspiring editorial team leader.

Steve Crabtree, our first-rate writer and reporter.

Jennifer Robison, our remarkably prolific senior editor and world-class writer, reporter, and interviewer.

Yvonne Sen, publishing specialist, and Eric Nielsen, senior director, media strategies, both outstanding professionals who lend their expertise to the *GMJ.*

Julie Fienhold, who plays a key role in supporting Gallup's internal customers, and Tony Marfisi, who does an excellent job producing *GMJ* podcasts.

Molly Hardin and Brian Pope, who provide outstanding design and graphics for *GMJ* and the site's hardcopy reprints.

Beth Karadeema, for her elegant design and graphics for the book.

Julie Lamski, our outstanding project manager.

Stephanie Oswald, Mick Colon, Elizabeth Davies, Nick Grundmeier, Nate Hales, Mike Jaros, Matt Johnson, Kim Ideus, and Seth Warrick, the *GMJ's* cutting-edge and highly innovative technical team.

Piotr Juszkiewicz, Gallup Press' enormously talented and tireless associate publisher.

Jim Clifton, Gallup's chairman and CEO, and Larry Emond, Gallup's chief marketing officer and executive publisher of Gallup Press, both of whom offer unflagging support and visionary leadership.

And last but not least, all the Gallup associates who contribute to the *GMJ*'s success, from interviewers to researchers to copyeditors. We could not have published this book without their contributions.

LEARN MORE

To stay up-to-date on the latest insights into Gallup's research on employees, customers, brands, leadership, and organizational performance, visit the *Gallup Management Journal* at http://gmj.gallup.com, where management experts regularly contribute articles and company profiles.

Readers of *Decade of Change* can receive a six-month subscription to the Gallup Management Journal. Simply go to: www.gallupjournal.com/promo/, then follow these instructions:

Enter the promotional code **DecadeofChange**, then click **Continue**.

If you already have a *GMJ* subscription, log in to your account. Review the subscription information, and if it is correct, click **Subscribe**.

If you do not have a *GMJ* subscription, click **Create an Account** and enter the required information. Click **Submit Registration**. Review the subscription information, and if it is correct, click **Subscribe**.

Then log in to begin exploring the site.

ABOUT THE EDITORS

Geoffrey Brewer is the Editorial Director of Gallup Press, which publishes books and the *Gallup Management Journal*. He is the editor of numerous bestsellers, including the #1 *New York Times* bestseller *How Full Is Your Bucket?* and the #1 *Wall Street Journal* bestseller *StrengthsFinder 2.0*, which has sold more than 1 million copies. He was previously a contributing writer on management for *The New York Times* and is a seven-time recipient of the Jesse H. Neal Editorial Achievement Award from American Business Media. Brewer lives in Brooklyn, New York, with his wife, Regan Solmo, and their son, Henry.

Barb Sanford is the managing editor of the *Gallup Management Journal* and an editor for Gallup Press, where she has worked on the *New York Times* bestsellers *12: The Elements of Great Managing* and *How Full Is Your Bucket?*, among others. Sanford is actively involved in the International Association of Business Communicators and has served in leadership roles at the chapter and regional levels. She lives in Lincoln, Nebraska, with her husband, Howard, and daughter, Elizabeth.